AN
INNOVATOR'S
TALE

An Innovator's Tale

New Perspectives for Accelerating Creative Breakthroughs

Craig Hickman

John Wiley & Sons, Inc.

Published by John Wiley & Sons, Inc., New York.
Published simultaneously in Canada.

This publication is designed to provide accurate and authoritative
information in regard to the subject matter covered. It is sold with
the understanding that the publisher is not engaged in rendering
professional services. If professional advice or other expert
assistance is required, the services of a competent professional
person should be sought.

ISBN: 0-471-44388-3

10 9 8 7 6 5 4 3 2 1

❧ The Companies in ❧ An Innovator's Tale

Carter-Crisp Foods Company, Beverly Hills, California
Eight hundred million dollars in revenues, 3,200 employees, consumer products manufacturer (potato chips, corn chips, pretzels, crackers, dips, spreads, and sauces)

Nibblers Corporation, Los Angeles, California Thirty billion dollars in revenues, 174,000 employees, consumer products manufacturer (corn chips, potato chips, pretzels, dips, sauces, beverages, frozen foods, and prepackaged meals)

Dameco International AG, Frankfurt, Germany One hundred million dollars in revenues, 400 employees, manufacturing services provider (food product packaging and packaging technology development)

Barclays Corporation, San Diego, California Two and one-half billion dollars in revenues, 15,000 employees, online retailer (books, videos, music, and electronics)

HomeService, Inc., White Plains, New York Nine hundred million dollars in revenues, 21,000 employees, home delivery services provider (delivery of fast foods, pharmaceuticals, and groceries)

Zacharman Partners LLC, Chicago, Illinois Twenty-eight million dollars in revenues, 90 employees, advertising agency (consumer products and e-business)

Strategic Business Intelligence LTD, Chicago, Illinois Two hundred fifty million dollars in revenues, 600 employees, consulting services (competitor intelligence gathering and counter-surveillance)

Kibon, Ltda, São Paulo, Brazil Five hundred million dollars in revenues, 4,000 employees, consumer products manufacturer (ice cream and frozen desserts)

♣ The Players in ♣
An Innovator's Tale

Taylor Zobrist   Vice President of New Product Development for Carter-Crisp Foods (former Director of Marketing Research and Strategy Development for Carter-Crisp and part-time consultant)

Dieter Wilkins   Director of Product Innovation for Kibon (former Vice President of New Product Development for Carter-Crisp Foods)

Bob Casey   Vice President of Marketing for Carter-Crisp Foods

Nathan Goodrich   President and CEO of Carter-Crisp Foods

Tom Platt   Senior Consultant for Strategic Business Intelligence, Ltd.

Alex Bamus   Senior Vice President of Mergers and Acquisitions for Nibblers Corporation

Charlie Carter   Founder of Carter-Crisp Foods (deceased)

Mark Carter   Chairman of the Board of Directors for Carter-Crisp Foods (Charlie's eldest son)

Rosemary Carter   Member of the Board of Directors, Carter-Crisp Foods (Charlie's daughter)

William Carter   Member of the Board of Directors, Carter-Crisp Foods (Charlie's youngest son)

Ray Paulhamus   Member of the Board of Directors, Carter-Crisp Foods and personal attorney to the Carter family

Derek Jamison   Director of Marketing, Potato Chips, for Carter-Crisp Foods

3

THE PLAYERS IN *An Innovator's TALE*

Jon Chimura   Manager of Information Technology, New Product Development, for Carter-Crisp Foods

Kate Zobrist   Taylor's 11-year-old daughter

Jeremy Zobrist   Taylor's nine-year-old son

Jack Zobrist   Taylor's husband (deceased)

Eileen Stansbury   Taylor's mother

Angela Tavares   Dieter's girlfriend

Neil Zacharman   Founder and CEO of Zacharman Partners

Jim Martinez   Executive Vice President of Carter-Crisp Foods

Carly Makaron   Vice President of Human Resources for Carter-Crisp Foods

Fred Erickson   Vice President of Information Technology for Carter-Crisp Foods

Amy Grow   Taylor's administrative assistant

Martha Johnson   Goodrich's administrative assistant

Brad Strauss   Director of New Product Development, Packaging, for Carter-Crisp Foods

Carl Ramage   Manager, New Product Packaging

Gaspar Ferreira   Chairman and CEO of Nibblers Corporation

Alan Montgomery   Chicago Bureau Chief for the FBI

Heather   Casey's girlfriend

Michael Silva   Consultant and retreat presenter

Christopher Raia   Consultant and retreat presenter

Don Mangum   Consultant and retreat presenter

✤ Prologue ✤

*T*oday's business headlines paint a triumphant yet troubling picture of the postmodern workplace: accelerating business growth, widespread organizational obsolescence, staggering technological advancements, rampant corporate espionage, revolutionary product innovations, and a disturbing rise in the number of workers selling company secrets and sabotaging potential deals . . .

Today's Companies Won't Make It

Business concepts or business models are becoming obsolete at an accelerating pace. It's not only product life cycles that are shrinking; strategy cycles are shrinking. Companies are going to have to reinvent themselves much more frequently than before. Or die faster.

> Thomas A. Stewart and Gary Hamel
> *Fortune* Magazine

Create. Destroy. Create Again.

Dot-bombs. Dried-up IT spending. Layoffs. Bankruptcies. Liquidations. Bloodied stocks. If ever there was a time for late economist Joseph Schumpeter to make a comeback, the time is now. Schumpeter coined the phrase "gales of creative destruction" to describe the elemental force that drives capitalism and the creation of societal wealth. Schumpeter celebrated the entrepreneur. A hard realist, he also recognized that capitalism's dark side, its destructive force, is necessary to clear the ground so new ideas, new creation, can take root and grow. Business executives, being human, try to avoid the negative. They pretend they can innovate within their existing organizational structures without bearing the pain that accompanies transformational change."

William J. Holstein, Kim Girard,
Russ Mitchell, and Edward Luttwak
Business 2.0 Magazine

Organizations Are Disappearing

The short and the long of it: Organizations, as we have known them for hundreds of years, are disappearing. Literally. What the hell is an organization? It used to be about buildings. (Don't tell Alcoa.) About departments. About fat payrolls. Now . . . it seems that it's not. Buildings are tumbling. Boundaries are vanishing. Temps . . . with LLDs . . . are coming. Where "you" start and where "I" stop are no longer clear. Where "I" stop and where "you" start are no longer clear. How far will it go? Very far. F-L-A-T (disintermediated) orgs . . . the watchword of the 80s and 90s. F-L-A-T (disintermediated) value chain . . . the watchword of the late 90s and first decade of century 21. Then . . . F-L-A-T society (Ross Perot's electronic democracy, etc.)? Who knows?

Tom Peters
The Circle of Innovation

Chances Are, Somebody's Watching You

Surveillance is everywhere: streets, stores, banks, golf courses. But privacy advocates are not smiling for the cameras. . . .

Whether as motorists or pedestrians; as visitors to convenience stores, banks, ATMs, or the post office; as shoppers with credit cards or telephone users; even at leisure, in parks and playgrounds and golf courses, we're constantly on candid camera. Full-time surveillance is a reality of modern life.

M. J. Zuckerman
USA Today

Corporate Spies

Almost every Fortune 500 company these days has a *competitive intelligence* (or CI) unit or farms out its spy activities. Coca-Cola, 3M, Dow Chemical, General Electric, and Intel all maintain a staff dedicated to uncovering what business rivals are up to.

Adam L. Penenberg and Marc Barry
The New York Times

Dirty Tricks Are All in a Day's Work

Cheating in business, of course, is older than the wheel. But corporate spooks and saboteurs are especially busy in today's global, high-tech economy, where the most prized assets can be stored on a disk and surveillance equipment can fit on a shirt button. . . . The FBI has nearly tripled its investigations into corporate espionage in the past year. . . . In this era of downsizing and diminishing corporate loyalty, close to two-thirds of all U.S. intellectual property losses can be traced to insiders, according to Richard J. Heffernan, a Bradford, Connecticut, security consultant and coauthor of a biannual espionage survey by the American Society for Industrial

Security. "People are always looking for somebody who looks different, when a great deal of the theft is committed by insiders who walk and talk just like you and me."

Daniel Eisenberg
Time Magazine

Deals & Deal Makers

"So far this year world-wide, there have been more than 30,000 deals valued at $3 trillion in announced mergers, up from more than 27,000 deals valued at $2.54 trillion in the year-earlier period."

Steven Lipin and Nikhil Deogun
The Wall Street Journal

1
CHAPTER

he FedEx envelope for Taylor Zobrist arrived a little before 10 on Thursday morning. Taylor's assistant, Amy Grow, saw who it was from, stood immediately, made her way through the long maze of cubicles to her boss's office, and opened the door. Taylor looked up from the papers in front of her and made her irritation clear as she tucked a wayward strand of shoulder-length auburn hair behind one ear.

"I know you said no interruptions this morning," Amy explained, as she put the envelope in front of Taylor. "But I thought you'd want to see this right away." She pointed to the sender's name.

Taylor looked, and nodded slowly, but her heart had begun to race. "Thanks, Amy," she said coolly, watching to make sure Amy closed the door behind her.

Alone, she looked at the name again: Dieter Wilkins, New York, New York. Dieter Wilkins, Vice President of New Product Development for Carter-Crisp Foods—and her boss. The man hadn't been seen in over a week and if senior management knew where he was—if the rumors of his sudden resignation were true—they weren't saying a word. She picked up the envelope, sat back and, for a moment, just held it.

It had been a week of crazy days and late nights for Taylor, working like mad to finalize an important project for Dieter. It was the first major presentation that she'd been asked to make since joining Carter-Crisp Foods almost three months earlier as the director of marketing research and strategy development, and she knew that it had to be good. But making a good case to Nathan Goodrich, the company's president, for why the last two product-line introductions had failed, wasn't proving easy—or palatable.

No matter how she combined, organized, or emphasized the data, she still came to the same conclusion: The product lines—specially seasoned pretzels five months earlier, and gourmet popcorn only seven weeks ago—had failed because of Nibblers, Carter-Crisp's major competitor. With suspiciously flawless timing, Nibblers had introduced its own new lines of pretzels and popcorn just weeks before Carter-Crisp had.

For years, Carter-Crisp had enjoyed a substantial speed-to-market advantage over Nibblers when it came to introducing new products, and with annual sales at $800 million as compared with Nibblers' $30 billion, Carter-Crisp was more agile. Nothing added up, and for the hundredth time, a single, disquieting thought occurred to Taylor: Nibblers had a mole inside Carter-Crisp Foods. And for the hundredth time she chided herself for her cynicism, a mood she found herself retreating to with increasing frequency since her husband's death.

Taylor opened the package from Dieter Wilkins, hoping he had the answer she'd been looking for. Inside an envelope with her name and the word *confidential* stamped in red ink, was a single sheet of paper with a typed note on it.

Taylor:

I have resigned from the company. And, if management does what I think they'll do, you'll be my replacement. Unfortunately, I won't be around to help you through the transition, as I've left the country.

I've set up an e-mail account for us to communicate privately, but don't try to access the account from the office or your laptop. Go to the library on LaCienega or to Kinko's in the mall—anywhere you can get public access to the Internet. There'll be a message with more information waiting for you.

E-mail account: sedonawaitley@yahoo.com
Yahoo ID: sedonawaitley
Password: sedona

Destroy this note, and if anyone asks about the FedEx package, tell them it was a market research report from the advertising agency that I forgot to give you before I left. Check the e-mail message as soon as you can.

Good luck,
Dieter

Taylor folded the note in quarters, stuffed it and the envelope in her purse, and left her office.

"I'm taking an early lunch," she told Amy, hoping her anxiety was not obvious on her face. May 2, and already Los Angeles was too hot. Taylor perspired under her silk suit.

Amy raised her hand as the phone rang. She picked it up and then punched the hold button. "It's Martha Johnson," she said, "Nathan Goodrich wants to know if you can come to a meeting in the boardroom at five-thirty this afternoon."

"Did she say what the meeting was about?" Taylor asked and pictured Goodrich's administrative assistant; tall, thin, and tight-lipped. "Forget it. Just tell her I'll be there. I'll be back in an hour to finish up the presentation. Find out if the graphics department can have everything ready by four o'clock."

Taylor headed for the stairway and Beverly Boulevard. She didn't like feeling out of control, and Dieter's secretiveness made her feel just that way. Part of her—the no-nonsense, action-oriented part—wanted to walk into Nathan Goodrich's office right now, show him Dieter's letter, and ask what was going on. However, the other part—her more curious, less confident side—wanted to follow the thread to wherever it might lead.

In times of uncertainty, Taylor's mind always turned to what was most certain and precious in her life, her children, Kate and Jeremy. As she walked two blocks down Beverly Boulevard to LaCienega and entered the Beverly Center mall, she thought about how vulnerable they'd all become since Jack's death. But intrigue was intrigue, and a healthy dose of curiosity was fine Taylor assured herself as she went into Kinko's Copy Center; she'd see what Dieter had to say.

A Kinko's clerk escorted Taylor to one of the computers and logged her on. When he was gone, she typed in *www.yahoo.com* on the address line and waited for the web site to come up. Nervously, she looked around to see if anyone was watching, but the store was empty. Next, she clicked on the Check Mail icon; entered in the user name, *sedonawaitley;* and then typed in the password, *sedona*. There was one e-mail message in the inbox from Dieter Wilkins and she opened it.

Taylor:

Sorry for the clandestine routine, but after you read this you'll understand why. Goodrich and the rest of the management team think I've gone to work for Nestlé in Rio de Janeiro, but

I haven't, though I am in Brazil. I don't want anyone to know where I am, at least not until this whole thing blows over. People inside Carter-Crisp are passing information about new product development efforts to the competition. I know it sounds like a convenient excuse for the past two failures, but it's the only way Nibblers could have beat us to the market twice in a row. The numbers you've been working on should be evidence enough by now. I don't know who they are, but I suspect a handful of people inside Carter-Crisp and Nibblers are trying to sabotage the company's financial performance in order to force the Carter family to sell. This is the only explanation that makes sense. I'm sorry I can't say more, but please be careful. If you want to contact me, use the e-mail address attached to this message, but don't write it down—memorize it. And when you're done, erase the message. I don't need anyone tracking me down through my e-mail address, and you certainly don't need anyone knowing that you're communicating with me. Good luck, Taylor, I'll try to help you any way I can.

Dieter

Taylor read the message two more times, then erased it. She knew from experience, conducting her home-based consulting business, that e-mail was far from private. When she looked at her hands poised over the keyboard, she saw that they were shaking.

Out on Beverly Boulevard again, Taylor took the long route back to work, knowing that a good walk always helped her think straight. Dieter's message had confirmed what she'd already suspected: that Carter-Crisp's new lines had failed because of inside information. It was troubling, to say the least, and she sensed that Dieter wasn't telling the whole story.

Standing in front of Carter-Crisp's gleaming corporate headquarters, Taylor hesitated for a moment and thought of

Jeremy and Kate. It would be easy, maybe even smart, to simply not go back, to step away from all this. But Taylor Zobrist was not a woman who frightened easily or who backed away from a challenge. She'd survived Jack's death, and she'd worked hard to get where she was. As she entered the building, her only plan of action was to remain flexible.

2

CHAPTER

*T*aylor smoothed the skirt of her light gray suit, straightened the silver chain on her neck, and ran her fingers through her hair. She knew she looked less than calm. Though she had spent the afternoon refining her presentation on the failure of the company's recent product lines, Taylor suspected that her summons to the third-floor boardroom by Nathan Goodrich was for an entirely different reason. If Dieter was right, she would be asked to be his replacement, and now she wasn't at all sure that she wanted the job.

Regardless of her ambivalent feelings, Taylor knew she had no choice but to tell Goodrich the truth—though maybe not the whole truth. As she rehearsed what she would say one more time, it hit her. What if Goodrich was behind the sabotage?

Taylor entered the large, modern boardroom and waited for the three men standing at the far end to acknowledge her. It had been a year and three months since Jack's car accident and at times like this, she missed him more than she liked to admit. Even though she'd been working for Carter-Crisp and other clients from home for years as a part-time marketing consultant before becoming director of marketing research and strategy development, she was still nervous about interacting with three of the company's senior executives, still not always sure of herself. Her heart tightened and she took a deep breath. The men turned.

"Come on in, Taylor," Goodrich said, waving her in.

Taylor noted his craggy face and soft eyes. At 55, he still had the physique that had made him a college football star at USC in the 1960s. He offered Taylor his hand, and the two other men—Jim Martinez, Executive Vice President, and Bob Casey, Vice President of Marketing—came forward.

"You're probably wondering why we invited you here," Goodrich said, looking at the stack of overhead slides Taylor had brought with her. He sat at the head of the granite-topped table and motioned for Taylor to sit at his left, the other men opposite her.

Taylor smiled self-consciously. She was aware that men found her attractive, even with the spray of freckles across her nose and nascent wrinkles around her hazel-green eyes—the two things, she thought, that made her look every day of her 38 years. Too much Southern California sun, she reminded herself.

"Let me get right to the point," Goodrich said. "We're not here to have you give us a presentation. We'd like you to become our new Vice President of New Product Development, which brings with it an immediate forty-thousand-dollar raise in your annual salary and the opportunity to participate more fully in the company's profit-sharing and stock-option plans."

Taylor froze. Even though Dieter had prepared her for this, hearing the words from Nathan Goodrich's mouth made her light-headed.

"Dieter's taken a job with Nestlé in Rio de Janeiro," Goodrich said. "You know his girlfriend Angela's from there."

Taylor thought about Dieter, the way he'd mentored her as a consultant and then as a member of his management team, his difficult divorce, his fling with a Brazilian woman, and the near nervous breakdown he'd suffered a few weeks after the second new product line introduction failed so miserably. Most people thought he was burned out and needed a change of scenery; others, though, said he couldn't take the pressure from Goodrich and the Carter family to increase sales and profits from new products. Now, Taylor knew the real story, or at least part of it.

Though Goodrich had not yet asked Taylor if she'd accept the promotion, for the next 20 minutes, he detailed the challenges she would face in her new assignment. First, she'd have to revitalize the new product development division with an esprit de corps and results orientation that had been missing in recent months, which might mean firing a few people and hiring some new ones. Second, she'd need to discover why the company's new product introductions had been failing. Third, she'd have to make the necessary corrections. And fourth, she would need to introduce at least four new product lines during the next six months that would add $40 million in sales and $8 million in profits that year. Otherwise, Goodrich warned, the Carter family would resume its negotiations to sell Carter-Crisp Foods to the snack food giant and industry leader, Nibblers. When Goodrich finished, he raised his chin slightly and looked down his uneven nose at Taylor. "Can we count on you?"

Taylor leaned forward, hoping to discover in Goodrich's eyes that she could trust him. Wasn't this what she'd worked so hard for? Wasn't this about her children's future, too? "Of course you can," she said, suddenly. "I'm just a little overwhelmed at the moment."

"And we're all here to support you. Reviving the company's innovative spirit and its track record of successful new product introductions is critical to all of us," Goodrich said, turning to Casey and Martinez who nodded in agreement. "Carter-Crisp Foods used to be the leader in innovation. It's time we recapture that vision, no matter what it takes."

As Taylor studied Goodrich's face, the ruddy complexion and soft blue-green eyes, she wondered if this was the sort of friendly pressure that made it impossible for Dieter Wilkins to stick around. So why was she saying yes?

"We wouldn't be offering you this assignment if we didn't think you were capable of turning things around," Goodrich added, as though sensing her uncertainty. "We've done our homework on you, and the fact that you've been here just under three months is a plus, not a minus. Your fresh perspective is just what the new product development division needs. But what I'm telling you is, you don't have to do this by yourself. We're here to help you."

Taylor replayed Goodrich's words in her head as she drove home to Marina del Rey. Though she still had misgivings about her ability to turn things around as quickly as Goodrich and the Carter family expected, something inside her had persuaded her to trust Goodrich.

When she got home, Taylor sat in the den of her bayside condominium before calling her mother who had picked up Kate and Jeremy after school. Surrounded by the happy, comforting clutter that was life with kids, she gazed out the window at the ocean view and waited for calm to wash over her, but was instead overcome with sudden apprehension. She could not name or dispel it, and the effect was so chilling she began to shiver.

3

CHAPTER

As soon as he got back to his office, Bob Casey called Derek Jamison, one of five marketing directors who reported to him. "Goodrich just appointed Taylor Zobrist to take Dieter's place," he said, uneasily. He had expected Goodrich to pick someone else—someone who'd been with the company longer and was used to Casey's influence in the company. Even though Martinez, not Casey, had been recently promoted to executive vice president, Casey was the company's most powerful executive after Goodrich. Taylor was a wild card, and he didn't like it.

"What do you want to do?" Jamison asked.

"I want you to find out everything about her . . . and I mean everything. We can't afford to get blindsided with her promotion the way we did with Dieter's resignation."

"You got it," Jamison said. "Any word on Dieter?"

"Nothing. But don't worry, we'll find him."

After hanging up, Casey walked to the large window and admired his own reflection; the handsome well-tanned face, youthful for 40, thick black hair, and brown eyes. He deserved to be the next CEO of Carter-Crisp Foods, regardless of what the board thought. All he needed was 90 more days of declining sales and profits to force the Carter family, who owned 75 percent of the company, to sell Carter-Crisp Foods to the Nibblers Corporation. After that, he could sell his own 5 percent of the company to Nibblers, pocket another $5 million for making the deal, then take over as CEO of Nibblers' newest acquisition. And no one—especially a woman, a mother, who'd been working part-time for more than 10 years—was going to interfere with his plans.

He glanced at his watch. It was a little past seven and time to leave. It was his custom to drive his black Porsche 911 Turbo home each day to his beach house in Santa Monica, relax with a scotch and water in front of CNN, and then decide where and with whom he wanted to dine. He lived alone, except when he allowed one of his girlfriends to stay for a few days, and the nightlife in West Los Angeles was far too enticing to keep him in.

Tonight, though, an unusual restlessness overcame him. Of all the people Goodrich might have picked to replace Dieter Wilkins, Taylor Zobrist was the last person he'd expected. He finished his drink, walked into his opulent, cherrywood-paneled den, and turned on his computer. When the screen was up, he brought up a browser and ran a Dog-pile search on *private investigation*. He would be dining in tonight.

4

CHAPTER

It was early morning when Taylor called Thomas Ririe Platt in Chicago at his office. During a restless night, his was the name that kept popping into her head, though she hardly knew him. She had met Tom a few months earlier at a marketing and competitor intelligence conference, when she'd attended his workshop on countering the surveillance of competitors. She'd been impressed by him and his obvious authority on the subject.

As the phone rang, she recalled how she'd asked for his card, "Just in case I might need it some day." She had laughed at the idea then, but now it was startlingly serious. She found herself growing wistful in the early morning light, with her kids still asleep and the condo so quiet. How things had changed in such a short time.

"Hello?"

"Is this Thomas Platt?" she asked. "It's Taylor Zobrist. Marketing consultant. Or at least I was." She paused, wondering if he would remember her. "We met in Los Angeles during your countersurveillance workshop." Still no signs of recognition. "Last January at the Biltmore."

"I wish I could say I remember every single person who's attended one of my workshops, but I don't." Taylor heard him take a sip of something. "Taylor Zobrist, you do know it's Saturday, don't you? I'm not officially working today."

"I see," she laughed. "And that's why you're in your office."

Tom laughed in return. "And you're working, too, I assume. In that case, what can I do for you Taylor Zobrist?"

By the end of the conversation, during which Taylor had explained her situation and had convinced Tom to fly out to Los Angeles and have a meeting with her, she was sure he remembered her.

"Kate! Jeremy! Turn those cartoons off and come get the world's best pancakes!"

In a flash, her kids pounded into the kitchen, still in their pajamas, and by now very hungry. They talked, and as she watched them tease each other, she knew she was doing the right thing taking the promotion. With more money and the freedom she hoped corporate success would bring, she could create the kind of future for her children that she and Jack had always dreamed of.

It's all in how you look at the situation, she told herself, and this morning the situation looked pretty good. She speared a pancake, and took a bite big enough to make her kids erupt in laughter.

5

CHAPTER

athan Goodrich followed Charlie Carter's three children and their attorney into the boardroom and closed the door behind him. Goodrich had already prepared himself for the worst, and there was a definite somberness in the air as everyone took their places around the boardroom table. The five composed the board of directors of the privately held Carter-Crisp Foods Company and had convened to conduct their second quarterly board meeting of the year.

As Mark Carter, Charlie's oldest son and chairman of the board, called the meeting to order, Goodrich recalled the company's long and proud history. Carter-Crisp Foods had been founded in 1952 when Charlie obtained his first contract to produce private-label potato chips for a small chain of grocery stores in Southern California. Charlie had been a mentor to Goodrich and a man who had run his company with a firm hand and a warm heart up until the day he died 10 years ago. After Charlie's death, his three children—Mark, Rosemary, and William, all of whom had worked in the business growing up but eventually left to pursue other endeavors—inherited 75 percent of the business. The other

25 percent had been set aside for equity sharing with key executives—Goodrich himself owned about 12 percent, the rest was spread among the company's seven vice presidents.

The minutes of the last board meeting were read by Rosemary Carter and unanimously approved by the board. Then Mark turned the meeting over to his brother William who, for the past six months, had been handling negotiations for the sale of the company to Nibblers.

"Their latest offer is six hundred fifty million dollars, fifty million more than the last one. The deal remains basically unchanged, two hundred million dollars in cash and the rest in Nibblers' stock. Alex Bamus, our main contact at Nibblers, told me the executive committee is beginning to lose its patience with this deal. He said this would be their final offer. Frankly, I think we should take it. We'd never get this much in a public stock offering, at least not given the company's recent performance," William glanced at his brother and sister and then at Ray Paulhamus, their attorney.

The four of them exchanged looks and nodded in silent agreement, and then, as if choreographed, they turned to Goodrich who rose slowly from his chair and began pacing around the boardroom table.

"Remember what your father used to say about Nibblers? Corporate atheists. That's what he called them because they didn't believe in anything that couldn't be recorded on a balance sheet or income statement. He thought they were the worst thing that ever happened to the snack food industry, not just because they worshipped the bottom line, but because they were destroying the industry's creativity. Experimentation used to be the hallmark of this industry. Now it's called strategic innovation and it prevents any product with less than fifty million dollars in sales from staying on the shelves." Goodrich's voice rose. "That's how they destroy their competitors, by raising the bar so high we can't compete. And you're right, that's what they're doing to us. So why not sell before they bury us? I'll tell you why. Because there aren't many of us left, and if we give up, the others will, too. Whether there are three or twenty major competitors in our so-called non-vital industry may not make any difference to the Justice Department, but it makes a huge difference to our customers and our people and entrepreneurs like Charlie who might want to produce something other than software." He paused. "Look, you know where I stand on this. I've always been loyal to this family, and I'm not going to stop now. I'll accept whatever you decide, but if your father were here right now, you know he'd be saying the same things I am."

A heavy silence hung in the air. Nathan Goodrich had been a lifetime friend of the Carter family's, and he knew that everyone in the room considered him to be a man of loyalty and integrity. He'd been in the trenches building this company with Charlie for over 30 years and what he said mattered.

Mark Carter finally spoke. "You know we agree with you Nathan, but the longer we wait, the more we risk. We could lose everything our father worked for. He wanted his grandchildren and their children to benefit from his legacy and that's what we're trying to protect. And, I certainly don't have to tell you that the recent new product failures and Dieter Wilkin's sudden departure don't paint a pretty picture. I think it's time to cut our losses."

"Taylor Zobrist is one of the brightest new stars in this company. I think she can turn new products around," Goodrich said.

"She's been with the company for less than three months. How can we expect her to turn things around?" Rosemary said, cutting him off.

Goodrich looked directly at her. "She's good, Rosemary. We would have hired her years ago, but she only wanted to

work part-time, so she could raise her kids. Her husband died
a year ago in a car accident. That's why she returned to full-
time work. I promise you, if anyone can resurrect this company's innovative spirit, she can. I've got one of those feelings
about her." He knew that his greatest strength as an executive was his ability to select and develop good people, but now
he wondered if the people in the room thought he was wearing out, just like Charlie had worn out.

"Can she do it in three months?" William asked.

"I guarantee you she'll add fifty million dollars in sales
and ten million dollars in profits before our next board meeting," Goodrich said. His chest rose in a posture of certainty.
He had just promised more than he ever should have—he'd
told Taylor she'd have six months to increase sales by $40 mil-
lion and profits by $8 million—but these were desperate
times and he believed she could do it. And he was willing to
do whatever it took to support her.

"I could probably string Bamus out for another three
months, but after that, I think they'll withdraw the offer.
Then the doors will be closed forever. That's how they play
the game," William said.

"I can slow things down from my end. Estate trust issues,
taxes, that sort of thing. Let them think we're moving forward with the sale," Paulhamus offered.

More questions and concerns were raised during the next
90 minutes, but the board members had already made their
decision. Goodrich would have his additional three months.
His impassioned reasoning and long-term relationship with
Charlie had been enough to win the day. Now all he had to do
was deliver—and that meant getting Taylor Zobrist to deliver.

Later, when the board members had left Carter-Crisp
headquarters, Goodrich asked Martha to find Taylor Zobrist
and have her come to his office as soon as possible.

6
CHAPTER

ob Casey and Derek Jamison entered Bacardi's restaurant in Beverly Hills and were immediately seated at a table in a secluded window alcove overlooking Sunset Boulevard. After they ordered drinks and sushi, Casey got right to the point.

"What have you got?" he asked Jamison.

"She made contact with a man named Thomas Platt. He works for a consulting firm, Strategic Business Intelligence. Lives in Chicago. 40 years old. No wife. No family. He used to work for the National Security Agency."

"What?" Casey said abruptly as he put down his glass of water. "When did she contact him?"

"Saturday morning."

"Did you get the conversation?"

"We only know whom she calls and who calls her," Jamison explained. "We tried to get as much information on him as we could. The bugs will be in place by tomorrow."

"No," Casey said. "She knows something. Dieter must have contacted her."

"How? There's no evidence that happened."

"You have another explanation for her contact with this guy Platt? Check out his firm—find out exactly what kind of consulting he does." Casey took a gulp of water, but he'd lost his appetite. "Keep her under surveillance but hold on the bugs for now. I don't want someone to find them."

"If Dieter contacted her, he may have contacted others," Jamison suggested, looking anxiously around the restaurant. "Have we gotten any updates from Brazil about Dieter's location?"

"None. I'll call Bamus tonight to see if they can speed up the search," Casey said, sensing Jamison's growing nervousness. "We're really close, Derek," he said, leaning closer to the man. "The Board gave Goodrich one more quarter—then it's over. All we have to do is keep sales down. Fifty million dollars is their target; we can make sure they don't reach it. And when you feel yourself getting cold feet, just remember, we deserve this. It's ours." Casey paused to let his words sink in. "What else did you find out?"

"She's got two kids, a girl, eleven, and a boy, nine. Her husband, a respected corporate attorney, died in a nasty head-on collision with a drunk driver a little over a year ago. According to Amy, her assistant, Taylor worries about her children, thinks about them all day long. She didn't want to come back to full-time work, but she needed the benefits and the regular income. Her kids, obviously, are her soft spot. Her clients say she's brilliant. She's a conceptual thinker, strategically adept, has lots of market savvy, and seems to be quite gifted when it comes to marketing over the Internet. And she doesn't miss any details."

"Except when she's worrying about her kids," Casey suggested.

As the waitress arrived with their food, Casey followed her every move as she placed the platter of sushi and accompaniments in front of them. He winked and smiled at her when she was done.

Jamison shook his head, "You're incorrigible."

Casey's appetite was back. He gulped down a California roll and sipped his sake. "Is this Platt a boyfriend?"

"I don't think so. Word is she and her husband were very close—she's not looking for another relationship."

"What about siblings, parents, close friends?"

"Her mother lives in Santa Monica. No living brothers and sisters. Closest friend lives near London—teaching at Cambridge for the year."

"Good work, Derek," Casey said, still concerned about Jamison's nervousness. "Don't forget. We deserve this."

Casey sat back, reflecting for a moment. Goodrich had made too many promises that he couldn't keep—to promote Jamison to VP of marketing and Casey to executive vice president with the ultimate plan of making Casey CEO. But a year ago, the board had rejected the idea based on Casey's lifestyle. Promiscuous, they called it, irresponsible, a liability to the company's good name. Admittedly, he enjoyed his clubbing and one-night stands, but he never let them compromise his business judgment. Two years ago, after a bitter divorce from his second wife, he'd been arrested for marijuana possession, and the board had never forgotten it, even though the charges were eventually dropped. Casey had been preparing to take legal action against Carter-Crisp Foods when he met Alexander Bamus.

Over beers at Baci's, a high-end Westwood celebrity bar, the two of them commiserated about corporate politics, discrimination at senior executive levels, and the finer details of litigating against major corporations for unfair employee management practices. Bamus had recently been passed over for a group president position at Nestlé and was now working for Nibblers in Los Angeles. Casey was intrigued, and when he discovered that Bamus's new assignment at Nibblers was Senior Vice President of Mergers and Acquisitions, his head filled with ideas.

What ensued in the months after their first encounter was the development of a close relationship—Bamus's dining and clubbing tastes mirrored Casey's—and the hatching of a plan for Nibblers to acquire Carter-Crisp Foods. Their interests, it seemed, were unusually similar. Six months ago, after the Carter family rejected Nibblers' first offer to buy the company, Bamus and Casey started playing hardball: full-time surveillance on Dieter Wilkins.

"I've gotta get back for a meeting," Jamison said, interrupting Casey's reflection. He pushed back from the table.

"Keep on Taylor, and find out about Platt's line of consulting as soon as you can. I'd like to have that information before I call Bamus."

After Jamison left the restaurant, Casey called his assistant on his cell phone. "Keep your eye on Jamison, he's under a lot of pressure," he instructed her. "I'll be back in an hour or so." Casey checked his watch and looked around the room for his waitress. Paying his bill might take some time because he was determined to get her phone number before he left.

7
CHAPTER

aylor entered the Kinko's Copy Center near her condo a little before midnight and went to the service counter to request Internet access. Ever since her latest meeting with Goodrich that afternoon when she'd learned about the new requirements—$50 million in sales and $10 million in profits in three months—for keeping Carter-Crisp off the market, she'd thought of little else. She didn't want Nibblers to acquire Carter-Crisp anymore than Goodrich did. She'd worked for huge companies like Nibblers before, and she hated the office politics and aggressive style they often fostered. If the rumors about the recent Towers Perrin culture assessment were true, Nibblers was a toxically competitive place to work. Winning was everything, and employees were rewarded for outperforming one another. It was time to have a chat with Dieter—she needed his help and she hoped he'd check his e-mail, sooner rather than later.

After logging on and typing in the secret user name and password, Taylor discovered another message from Dieter. She opened it and began reading.

Taylor:

I've been thinking about who had the most access to our new product plans. The fact is, it could be almost anybody in the company. However, the only person in the department I can imagine doing something like this is Chimura. He's been angry at me and the company since I blocked his promotion to director. He works for the Information Technology department but he's assigned to support New Product Development, so he really had two bosses—me and Fred Erickson. People who work with him complain that they can't trust him because he shades the truth. He's not a team player, but he has superb technical skills. He installed and currently maintains the company's e-mail system and Internet servers. That's what worries me. He has access to a lot of inside information. I don't know if he's capable of outright sabotage, but I thought you should know about him.

Dieter

Taylor wrote back immediately.

Dieter:

Thanks for the heads-up about Chimura. I'll keep an eye on him. You were right—they offered me your job and I accepted. According to Goodrich, the company will be sold in three months unless sales from new products reach $50 million with profits of $10 million before the end of the quarter. The board has singled out new product development because they think it's the key to the company's future—either we regain our product innovation edge or the company gets sold. Right now, I doubt there's any way we can deliver that level of results in such a short period of time, and I know we can't if somebody's leaking everything we do to Nibblers. I need two things from you as soon as possible: First, a list of *all* the contract manufacturers you've ever dealt with or know about, along with your assessment of their strengths and weaknesses; and second, your priorities for new product development if you were here, now, in my situation. Hope to hear from you soon. We don't have much time.

Taylor

Taylor waited an hour to see if Dieter might respond. When he didn't, she erased her tracks and logged off the computer. As she paid the Kinko's sales clerk, she realized that the past hour had been nothing more than a futile exercise in wishing and hoping for deliverance. Dieter wasn't going to solve her problem—he'd already removed himself from the challenge—and even if his input proved valuable, she was still the one who would have to make it happen. She'd have to inspire her people, unite them behind a near impossible innovation agenda, and then accelerate their breakthroughs to reach the expected results in 90 days. The reality struck her hard as she drove home.

If she was really going to go through with this, she'd have to resolve herself to it, completely, no reservations, no looking for an easy way out. If not, she ought to get out now, and find another job.

8

CHAPTER

om Platt arrived at LAX late Tuesday afternoon, obtained a rental car, and drove to the Carter-Crisp headquarters building in Beverly Hills. He signed in at the reception desk, attached his visitor badge to the lapel of his navy blue blazer, and walked over to the large glass display case of Carter-Crisp snacks—Golden Crisp Potato Chips, Los Hermano's Tortilla Chips, Carter's Country Baked Pretzels, Beverly's White Cheddar Popcorn, Carter's Cheeseboard Crackers, and a variety of dips, spreads, and sauces.

Amy Grow met Tom in the lobby and took him to Taylor's office.

"Tom. It's good to see you again," Taylor said as she stood up from the large cherrywood desk in her new office. She had been anxiously waiting for him, and now a sense of relief came over her. Tom was tall and rugged looking but not noticeably handsome. She remembered from their first meeting, the air of self-confidence about him that reminded her of her husband Jack. Already, she felt reassured by his presence.

"Good to see you, Taylor," Tom said as he shook her hand.

"Before we start, do you want to sweep the office or do whatever you do to make sure no one's eavesdropping?"

Taylor asked. She'd told him on the phone that critical new product information had been leaked to a competitor. Surely he hadn't forgotten.

"I would already know if someone were listening," he said, patting the slight bulge beneath the breast pocket of his blazer. Then he opened his brief case and pulled out a small, gray box the size of a cell phone. "But if it makes you feel better, I'll set up a shield." Tom stood and walked to the electrical outlet on the wall near the door. "This turns the electrical wiring in the walls of the room into an inhibiting shield. But if someone has you under surveillance, they probably already know who I am and have automatically assumed that your former boss has been in contact with you."

His comment unsettled her. He had remembered the details, but what he was telling her was not comforting. "So there's nothing we can do to stop them?"

Tom looked at her without speaking. Finally, he said, "No. We can protect you and counter their surveillance whenever we uncover it, but if someone with sufficient resources is determined to find out what you're doing and how you're doing it, they will. Unless, that is, you're willing to fundamentally change the way you live and work."

Tom continued. "I have a surveillance team I work with in Southern California. They'll need to have access to the entire building for about six hours tonight. After that, the building will be clean and they'll keep it that way for as long as you want. The problem is not monitoring surveillance devices, it's monitoring your people. If one of them is passing information to the competition—and, as I told you at the workshop in January, it happens more often than you'd think these days—the only thing we can do is catch him or her in the act."

"What did you mean about fundamentally changing the way I live and work?" Taylor asked.

Tom went through a litany of procedures—background checks, security precautions, communication protocols, and isolation techniques.

"All I want to do is get my new products to market without Nibblers undercutting us," Taylor said, her head spinning. "Can you help us stop them?"

"I can if you and your people are willing to put up with us until we discover the source and extent of the information leaks."

"How much will it cost?"

"Between two hundred and three hundred thousand dollars for every month we're involved."

"That's a problem. I can't approve that level of spending without going to the full executive team, and for all I know, one or more of them could be involved in this mess." Taylor felt her panic rise. She was in over her head, and she knew it.

"What level of spending *can* you approve?"

"Under one hundred thousand dollars per vendor per month. But we're going to need you for at least three months, which means six hundred to nine hundred thousand."

"At the end of three months, if you get your new products to market without any information leaks, do you have any reason to believe that your company will not honor its remaining financial obligation to us?"

"No. I'll need to inform our CEO that we're beefing up security, but he won't have a problem. I trust him," she said, hoping that her intuition about Goodrich's trustworthiness and willingness to support her was well founded.

"Then we'll invoice you ninety-nine thousand dollars a month for as long as it takes to pay off the bill," Tom said. "Now, are you ready to take me through a detailed review of the situation?"

Later that night, Platt's team of specialists met with Carter-Crisp's head of security to make a routine surveillance check of the building as part of a new privacy protection policy whenever senior-level people left the company. Taylor had been able to convince Goodrich and the company's human resources vice president, Carly Makaron, that such a policy was overdue at Carter-Crisp. Tom's suggestion that the functional department of the exiting executive be billed for the cost had made it easier for Makaron to agree.

Four hours later, Platt's team exited the headquarters building on Beverly Boulevard without finding a single bug. What they did find, however, as Taylor was informed later that night, were in-house Internet servers and e-mail systems with grossly inadequate security—meaning that a nominally sophisticated hacker could easily gain access to the computer and e-mail files of anybody in the company.

"Most companies don't realize how vulnerable they are to e-mail espionage," Tom said as he spoke to Taylor over her home phone line, which his people had already checked and found clean. "And if you get the wrong people working in your IT department, the ramifications can be severe. A company's entire operation can be undermined without the senior leadership knowing anything about it."

Platt's words caused Taylor's body to stiffen. She remembered Dieter's e-mail and the heads-up about Chimura. She thanked Platt and asked him to meet her at the office first thing in the morning.

9

CHAPTER

he next morning, Taylor took immediate action on three fronts: (1) correcting the company's IT security problem, (2) handling Jon Chimura, and (3) preparing for a four-day retreat with her key managers. First, she tracked down Fred Erickson—the 62-year-old soon-to-retire vice president of IT—to discuss the security level of the company's Internet servers and her concerns. The unscheduled meeting went on for more than an hour before Taylor could extract a commitment from Erickson to meet with Tom Platt as an initial step to correcting the problem. She also confirmed Dieter's suspicions about Jon Chimura. According to Erickson, Chimura not only lacked leadership and team commitment skills, he'd also become more and more secretive and recalcitrant in recent weeks. It wasn't difficult for Taylor to extract another commitment from Erickson to have Chimura fired.

Next, she went to Carly Makaron's office. Five years ago, Carly had been brought in to modernize Carter-Crisp's human resources function. She had been instrumental in increasing the percentage of women in management positions from 3 to 28 percent, and she'd been a major supporter among the executive team of Taylor's promotion. Taylor informed Carly of Platt's findings and her meeting with Fred Erickson. Then, she turned her attention to Chimura. "What do we have to do to fire Jon Chimura?"

"Ooooo," Carly said, making a face. "That's not going to be easy. He's one of our high potential candidates slated for promotion."

"Then why was he passed over for director last year?"

"If we'd promoted him last year, there would have been at least ten other highly competent managers in the company complaining that they were better qualified. We just couldn't justify it. Between us, Dieter nor I felt that Chimura had demonstrated the necessary leadership and judgment for a director-level job. Technically, he's brilliant, but his people management and team commitment skills still need developing. We felt he needed another two years of experience and growth."

"So there's documentation in his personnel file about this?" Taylor asked.

"Not the kind of documentation you need to fire someone," Carly said bluntly. Taylor sensed a growing tension between them. She needed Carly's help, but she couldn't tell her the real reason she needed to fire Chimura—at least not until she knew she could trust her.

"I know we don't know each other that well," Taylor said, "but I need you to trust me on this one. Chimura needs to be removed from the company as soon as possible. I'm planning a four-day retreat with the department's management team for next week. Ordinarily, he would be involved, but I can't have him there." She waited for Carly Makaron to respond.

After a long silence, Carly asked a question that made

Taylor shiver. "Does this have anything to do with your security concerns?"

Though thrown, Taylor had anticipated Carly making the connection. Trusting another member of the executive team besides Goodrich wasn't going to be easy. "Yes," Taylor said.

"Dieter talked to me about it a couple of weeks ago. I'll tell you the same thing I told him. We can't fire an employee on the basis of suspicions. We have to have evidence of wrong-doing."

Taylor composed her thoughts carefully and deliberately. "The last thing I want to do is communicate to Chimura or anyone else in the company that he's being fired for security reasons."

Carly sat back in her tan chair and rubbed her neck below her short sandy, grey hair. "I'll prepare the paperwork based on his leadership and team commitment ratings and his reluctance to receive and embrace developmental guidance. If you're right about him, the company will have no wrongful or discriminatory termination risk—but, if you're wrong, prepare yourself for a lawsuit. One thing Chimura does not lack is tenacity."

For the next 20 minutes Taylor and Carly hammered out the details of Chimura's termination. As Taylor returned to her office, she questioned whether she was doing the right thing by Chimura, the company, her career, her children. An hour later, she asked Amy to find Jon Chimura and invite him to her office as soon as possible.

Taylor was direct and to the point: She was building a new team of players and Chimura didn't qualify.

"Based on what?" Chimura said, defiantly, his hands in front of him on the conference table.

"Based on recent performance evaluations that document your lack of team commitment and a pattern of unwillingness to respond to constructive feedback and guidance."

"You may want to think twice about doing this to someone like me," Chimura said.

Taylor tensed, prepared for confrontation. "I'm sorry, but your employment here is no longer a matter of discussion. Our decision has been made. We're prepared to offer you six months' salary if you leave immediately and sign this release." She placed the single sheet of paper she and Carly had prepared in front of him.

Chimura read the statement and then pushed it back. "It's going to cost you more than that. Either you give me a year's salary or I'll get an attorney and sue the company for unjust cause."

Taylor was stunned by his aggressiveness but remained calm. Maybe she had made a terrible mistake. "This is a very generous—."

He cut her off. "You do whatever you want to, Ms. Zobrist. But if I don't get a check for $90,000 within a week, I'll sue you, and it'll end up costing you a lot more than ninety thousand." He got up from his chair and walked out.

Taylor went immediately to Carly's office to report what had happened. After calling security to monitor Jon Chimura's final exit from the building, Carly closed the door to her office and sat down. "Do you still think you did the right thing?"

A long silence hung in the air while Taylor searched her soul. Then, quietly but firmly she said, "I do."

"That's good enough for me, Taylor. I'll approve the year's salary as severance and have it hand-delivered to him after he signs the release."

Taylor left Carly's office shaken but grateful for the vote of confidence. She hoped this would be the end of her concerns about Chimura. When she returned to her office, Taylor immersed herself in planning for the location, agenda, outside presenters, and desired outcome of her four-day strategy retreat. Taking her directors and managers away from the office for four days was a big investment in time and money, she told herself, but if she planned it right, she could create an accelerated solutions environment that could make all the difference in her department's ability to deliver the necessary breakthroughs and results on schedule.

10

CHAPTER

*D*ieter Wilkins and his girlfriend Angela Tavares had just finished dinner at Gero's, their favorite restaurant located in the exclusive Jardims area of São Paulo. This was the neighborhood where Angela had grown up and where she and Dieter lived in a high-rise condominium. For that reason alone, Dieter felt comfortable, but he had also fallen in love with São Paulo's perfect climate, friendly people, and spectacular urban foliage, especially in the Jardims region below Avenida Paulista.

He'd always been a passionate man, open to new experiences and opportunities to give his heart away—it was one of the traits that had made him such a successful innovator at Carter-Crisp—but he'd been concerned about adapting to life in another country, especially a so-called third-world country. Fortunately, he found living in the Jardims to be not only first world, but in quality of life and friendliness, well beyond first world. Dieter and his two younger sisters had grown up in the United States, but their German mother and British father had given them the opportunity to travel to every continent on the globe. Brazilians were easily the most positive, amiable people he'd ever encountered, a people who seemed naturally disposed to following their hearts without any regrets. It was what gave the Brazilian culture its carefree, carnival-like flair—as well as its problems with drug addiction and sexually transmitted diseases. Nonetheless, Dieter was happy to be living in this sanctuary with the woman he loved. Even his new job as *diretor de produtos novos* for Kibon was turning out to be more interesting and challenging than he'd expected. And his Portuguese was getting better every day. Within six months—given the personalized tutoring he was receiving from Angela—he expected to be fluent in the language. Life was good and the future looked even better.

Dieter and Angela exuded happiness as they walked hand in hand along the charming, tree-lined streets toward their condominium. At 43, Dieter was balding and trying to get rid of a pot belly, and Angela, at 31, was strikingly beautiful, from her long brunette hair and bright eyes down to her tanned and carefully pedicured toes. Dieter told himself that it wasn't unusual to see older men with younger women, especially when they were rich men who lived in the Jardims. It had taken two years for Dieter to start dating again after his wife of a decade left him for a Hollywood producer. He'd wanted to have children while she'd wanted to pursue her fledgling acting career. Eventually, the love they once had was extinguished by the bickering. Now, with a new life in Brazil, removed from the growing complexities and pressures of corporate life in the Northern Hemisphere, Dieter was ready to ask Angela to marry him. He knew she wanted to have children as much as he did.

When they reached their building, the security guard behind the bullet-proof glass pushed the button to release the lock on the gate. They ascended the stone steps which ran through immaculate gardens to the elevator. As they got off

46

at the 15th floor and entered the foyer of their 3,000-square-foot condominium, Angela screamed, "*Que isso?*"

The place had been ransacked. Angela ran to the bedroom where she kept her jewelry in a small wall safe. She opened it and thoroughly examined the contents of each drawer. Nothing was missing. She cried out to Dieter, "*Nada foi robada.*"

Dieter had run to the den where he kept his business files and important papers. Everything was gone—his files, his books and loose-leaf binders, his laptop computer, even his data backup CDs. A single disturbing thought entered his head: The conspirators at Nibblers and Carter-Crisp, 5,000 miles away in another country, were still looking for information. Was it possible? Would they ever leave him alone? He thought about the e-mail he'd sent to Taylor the day before. Somehow, someone had read it and the others he'd sent, he surmised, and then used them to track him down. He'd been so careful, but obviously, that hadn't been enough. Or, maybe they were watching Taylor more closely than she realized. He suddenly admitted to himself that despite his efforts to help her and salve his own conscience, he may have only made things worse.

Angela ran into the den. "*Não. É impossível,*" she screamed as she placed both hands over her mouth in horror.

Dieter shuddered with fear. He took Angela in his arms and hugged her. It was the first time he really considered that their lives might be in danger. And that meant Taylor's, too.

11

CHAPTER

aylor arrived at the Four Seasons resort hotel at the foot of the Santa Ynez Mountains in Santa Barbara, California, Monday afternoon and checked into her room. The red roof tiles, ivory adobe, and graceful archways of the classic Spanish Colonial resort were perfect, she thought, for the sort of creative thinking and accelerated solutions she wanted to achieve in the next four days of the retreat. She still had some polishing to do on her presentation for that evening's kickoff. She wanted to create just the right tone for the five directors who reported to her and the 19 managers who reported to them. After unpacking her bags, she called the hotel operator for Tom Platt's room.

"Everything's secure," he told her, "and my team will be here until you leave Friday night."

Taylor appreciated, more than she could express at the moment, the sense of security Tom gave her. In fact, she thought, it was the safest she'd felt in a long time. She toyed with the idea of having dinner with Tom, to get to know him better, then she thought about Jack. They were a lot alike, Jack and Tom, but she knew Tom was single and reminded herself that she wasn't ready for that kind of relationship.

"I'll be in and out over the next few days, but my team will be in constant contact with me," Tom continued, "you have the number I gave you, in case there's an emergency."

Taylor wanted to talk with him about Dieter but decided to wait until she checked the e-mail account again. Yesterday, when she'd looked, there was still no message. It had been five days and she was worried about him. If she didn't hear something by tomorrow, she decided, she'd talk to Tom about it. But for now, she needed to turn her full attention to the retreat and the overview she would be presenting in just a few hours.

Tonight she would ask 24 people—people with families—to put their personal lives on hold for the next 90 days in order to come up with a handful of breakthrough innovations that could generate $50 million in revenue and $10 million in profit within three months. Even though the revenue and profits only had to be booked by the end of the quarter—shipped to retailers, not necessarily sold to consumers—it would still demand a superhuman effort and a lot of inspiration. Otherwise, they'd all be working for Nibblers at this time next year. That is, if they were all lucky enough to keep their jobs; Taylor knew Nibblers' reputation for big layoffs after an acquisition.

What made matters even tougher was the fact that Taylor needed her people to think and imagine differently than they ever had before. She knew this was difficult, even for the most devoted and responsive employees. But she had no choice other than to proceed in the only way she knew how. She'd learned from experience that innovation had more to do with altering perceptions than anything else, and that's exactly what she needed her people to do.

Such mental versatility came naturally for Taylor, but she realized that most people—even new product development types—did not have the same broad range of conceptual-practical cognitive capacity that she did. Her husband used to call it her extra dose of bandwidth and focusdepth. She liked the terms so much that she began using them with her clients.

The term *bandwidth* identified the range of strategic alternatives considered during innovation. *Focusdepth* identified the scope of organizational implications evaluated during innovation. Taylor regularly advised her clients that, in general, innovations fail to be realized or fall short of expected results for one of two reasons: (1) narrow bandwidth (i.e., the consideration of only a narrow range of strategic alternatives when coming up with the innovation) or (2) limited focusdepth (i.e., the evaluation of a limited scope of organizational implications when deciding how to implement the innovation). Developing greater bandwidth and focusdepth in her people in four short days at the Santa Barbara Four Seasons resort— notwithstanding its great vistas and lush surrounding—was going to take more than a miracle, it was going to require her department to embrace a whole new approach to innovation, one that could accelerate the necessary breakthroughs. Otherwise, they'd never meet the board's demands.

A concept from Richard Foster and Sarah Kaplan's book, *Creative Destruction: Why Companies That Are Built to Last Underperform the Market—and How to Successfully Transform Them,*[1] came to mind and she wrote it down:

> When in pursuit of innovation, most companies fail to clear the ground of strategic biases, cultural traditions, stifling processes, and resistance to new perspectives before they begin.

That's where she'd start her presentation.

---

[1] Foster, R., and S. Kaplan. *Creative Destruction: Why Companies That Are Built to Last Underperform the Market—and How to Successfully Transform Them.* New York: Currency-Doubleday, 2001.

As Taylor continued reviewing her notes, she high-lighted the quotes from Clayton Christensen. Among the thousands of business consultants, professors, and authors attempting to enlighten the current generation of managers and leaders on the subject of breakthrough innovation, none had more thoroughly identified and defined the problematic nature of innovation in business than Harvard Business School professor Clayton Christensen in his book, *The Innovator's Dilemma: When New Technologies Cause Great Firms to Fail.*[2] Christensen described the innovator's dilemma as follows: "the logical, competent decisions of management that are critical to the success of their companies are also the reasons why they lose their positions of leadership." In other words, if management defines the future too much in terms of the present, they will eventually get blindsided; on the other hand, if management spends too much time inventing the future, they will inevitably neglect the present. Either way, they lose.

The solution, according to Christensen, was for executives and managers to learn how to "simultaneously do what is right for the near-term health of their established businesses, while focusing adequate resources on the disruptive technologies that ultimately could lead to their downfall." Not only did she need to focus her team on hammering out the necessary product line extensions (i.e., pushing existing product lines to the next step by adding new seasonings, new packaging, and new promotions to increase sales), she also needed her team to create a new future by getting them to consider a dimension of innovation

---

[2] Christensen, C. *The Innovator's Dilemma: When New Technologies Cause Great Firms to Fail.* Boston: Harvard Business School Press, 1997.

McKinsey & Company consultants called "Horizon 3." She'd worked on a client project with the McKinsey consultants, who wrote *The Alchemy of Growth*[3]—Mehrdad Baghai, Stephen Coley, and David White—and planned to present their concept of three horizons for growth in her presentation. According to the authors, Horizon 1 encompassed "businesses that are at the heart of an organization—those that customers and stock analysts most readily identify with the corporate name." Horizon 2 comprised "businesses on the rise: fast-moving, entrepreneurial ventures in which a concept is taking root or growth is accelerating. Horizon 3 contained "the seeds of tomorrow's businesses—options on future opportunities." The idea was for a company to develop business innovations in all three horizons concurrently, not sequentially, in order to always keep the pipeline of innovations full and flowing, and the business growing at a healthy rate.

The problem was that Taylor needed sales and profits from all three horizons within 90 days. Even the most creative McKinsey consultants and most imaginative Harvard Business School professors would never consider tackling such a challenge, Taylor knew, but the thought motivated her even more. If she could pull this off, it would secure her future, and her children's futures—and make her a major player, even CEO material.

Before taking a shower and dressing for dinner and her presentation, Taylor reviewed the graphic that she'd been tweaking since yesterday.

The key to the graphic, Taylor told herself, was the idea that four different perspectives had to be developed and

---

[3] Baghai, M., S. Coley, and D. White. *The Alchemy of Growth*. Cambridge, MA: Perseus Publishing, 2000.

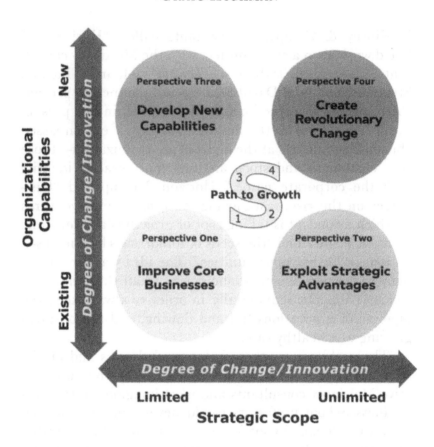

applied simultaneously—she called it the *S path to growth through innovation*. The graphic was her attempt to combine all the different aspects and levels of innovation that she'd been wrestling with over the past few days. Perspective One addressed Christensen's near-term, existing product focus and McKinsey's incremental innovation in Horizon 1. Perspectives Two and Three addressed Christensen's longer-term, disruptive technologies; McKinsey's more substantial and transforming innovations in Horizon 2; and Taylor's bandwidth and focusdepth concepts intended to broaden and deepen innovative thinking. Perspective Four addressed McKinsey's revolutionary innovations in Horizon 3 and Foster and Kaplan's concept of creative destruction as the key to fundamental and radical breakthroughs.

In addition, her four perspectives included the dimensions of strategic scope (limited or unlimited) and organizational capabilities (existing or new), which made the distinctions between types and levels of innovation more meaningful and easier to understand and apply. Perspective One was an incremental perspective that focused on stretching the brand or product line as far as it could go without effecting major changes in strategic scope or organizational capabilities. Perspective Two was an insightful perspective that transported the brand or product line to new customers and markets beyond the current strategic scope without making major changes in organizational capabilities. Perspective Three was an inventive perspective that deepened customer satisfaction and loyalty to the brand or product line by adding new organizational capabilities without introducing major changes in strategic scope. Perspective Four was an ingenious perspective that transcended the brand or product line to orchestrate fundamental changes in both strategic scope and organizational capabilities. Taylor thought of them as the four *I*s of innovation: *i*ncremental, *i*nsightful, *i*nventive, and *i*ngenious.

Her plan for the retreat was to spend one day on each of the four perspectives. Now, if she could just get her people to buy it. Tonight's speech would be her first opportunity to find out.

12

CHAPTER

ob Casey walked into Baci's Ristorante in Westwood near the UCLA campus and went immediately to the bar where he ordered a double Cutty neat. Tonight it would take more than the usual scotch and water to cut the rising tension he was feeling. For a fleeting moment, he wished he'd never met Alex Bamus or hatched their scheme to force the Carter family to sell Carter-Crisp Foods. Things had gotten more complicated than he'd expected, and they were now on the verge of becoming dangerous.

As Casey took his first drink and tried to relax, Bamus joined him at the bar. After ordering a beer, Bamus suggested they move to a quiet corner where they could talk privately.

"My people found Dieter," Bamus said, after they'd climbed onto their stools and set their drinks on their small round table. "He's living in the Jardims area of São Paulo. There was nothing in his apartment. We're still trying to retrieve whatever we can from his computer. So far, there's no evidence of any contact with Taylor."

"Nothing?"

"Give us some time. We're still going through his computer files. He was using AOL to access the Internet, but I doubt he'd use AOL's e-mail service or his own computer to contact Taylor. It's too risky, and he knows it," Bamus said. "What about Taylor's retreat?"

"We're locked out," Casey said. "She's got this former NSA operative providing protection. If we try to infiltrate, we run the risk of being discovered. Chimura was fired before he was able to get anything substantial on the retreat. Dieter must have alerted her about him."

"Or her NSA boy uncovered him. Either way, looks like we have no choice but to turn up the heat," Bamus said, without hesitation. "So the question is, when and how?"

Casey emptied the rest of his glass in a single gulp. "On the last day of the retreat we're going to send Taylor a message through her children," he said. He gestured to the waitress for another drink.

Bamus looked skeptical. "Are you absolutely sure there'll be no way to trace it to us?"

"We've already talked about this, Alex. You worry about Dieter. I'll take care of Taylor," Casey said. "We're not going to hurt anyone, just scare her. And don't worry, there won't be any link to *you*," Casey responded.

The noise from the bar invaded the silence that hung between them. Finally, Bamus got up and placed a $10 bill on the table. "Sure you wanna go through with this?" he asked, but continued before Casey could answer. "The probability that Taylor will meet the board's new numbers can't be more than twenty, thirty percent. Maybe you should wait."

"No, I'm not willing to wait and see. Not when we're this close," Casey said with renewed resolve.

"Let me see if I can put some more pressure on William. I'll tell him Nibblers' Executive Committee doesn't like the idea of waiting three more months. If the Carter-Crisp board doesn't bite in a day or two, you can go ahead as planned," Bamus said as he left Casey sitting alone in the corner of the busy bar.

Casey watched Bamus leave and then he surveyed the 30 or so women spread throughout the bar. He was not about to go home alone tonight.

13

CHAPTER

*A*fter a breakfast buffet in the gardens, Taylor's team assembled in the La Bella Vista room to begin their first full day focusing on Perspective One innovations. Last night her presentation had been received with keen enthusiasm, now the real work was about to begin. She hoped the enthusiasm would continue.

This first day would be the most grueling of the four, Taylor thought as she watched her team take their seats behind the long tables organized in a semicircle. Because of the short 90-day window, she'd already decided that 50 percent of the new revenues and profits ($25 million in sales and $5 million in profits) would have to come from Perspective One's incremental innovations, and that meant the sources would have to be identified by the end of the day.

Perspective One was the beginning of the **S** path to growth and represented those innovations that could be implemented rapidly and inexpensively (i.e., Improve Core Businesses). This included new and improved product variations, more convenient packaging, and modifications in other features (referred to as *product line extensions*). Most of Taylor's former clients referred to the type of innovation in Perspective

One as *milking the brand*. It didn't necessarily mean harvesting a cash cow (which is where the term *milking* originated), but it did mean stretching the brand or the product line as far as it could go without introducing major changes in terms of strategic scope or organizational capabilities.

The morning unfolded slowly as the team discussed and debated, often heatedly, a wide range of potential Perspective One innovations. As Taylor observed the interaction, she couldn't help wonder about the security of their meeting and whether there was a mole in the group. What if Chimura wasn't the only one? If there was someone else, she prayed Tom would be able to unmask him or her before any more damage was done.

Twenty-five different innovations were identified by the first break at 10:30. By noon, they had whittled the list down to 10 and were obviously ready for a lunch break. But Taylor had other plans. Knowing that the first day would be long and demanding, Taylor had made the decision to have lunch brought into the conference room so the team could keep working. It was her plan to symbolically communicate that the next 90 days were going to be grueling. After announcing the working lunch, she promised the group that tomorrow would be less of a crank-it-out day and would focus more on the creative. As soon as she said the words, she reminded herself to stop apologizing for the rigorous schedule, it was only going to get worse.

During lunch the new product team cut their innovation options down to six major initiatives capable of generating the needed $25 million in sales and $5 million in profits within the next 90 days: (1) an extra-cheese nacho chip, (2) a heavy-duty barbeque potato chip, (3) a miniature pretzel pack to price under $0.50, (4) a resealable chip package, (5) a larger snack assortment pack for schools and club stores, and (6) a two-for-one promotion package on all canned and bottled salsas, spreads, and dips. All six innovations had already undergone at least some preliminary research—it was one of the criteria for making it onto the short list—and were scheduled for implementation over the next two years. But now, they'd have to be implemented immediately and all at once, without additional research. It was a big risk and Taylor knew it, but under the circumstances, the company had no choice.

After lunch, the team broke up into six groups to hammer out detailed implementation plans, including sales and profit margin forecasts. Finally, at 8:00 that evening, the last of the six groups finished presenting and receiving critiques on its plan. Before adjourning for the day and partaking in a late dinner buffet, Taylor added up the expected sales and profit increases—$22 million and $4.6 million, respectively.

She breathed a sigh of relief when the group unanimously agreed to champion all six projects through the implementation process, which would mean getting the rest of the organization on board. There was still another $28 million in sales and $5.4 million in profits to be achieved, but today had been successful, she told herself as she walked with her team to the lavish buffet in the main dining area of the resort. One step at a time, she said quietly to herself—it was the only way she could think about it.

Before entering the dining room, she slipped into a phone booth to call her children. The next 90 days were going to be the hardest for them because they'd see little of their mother. Taylor was making a choice, but they had none. She couldn't help asking herself again, if she was doing the right thing by staying at Carter-Crisp.

14

CHAPTER

oodrich loosened his tie as he paced back and forth in front of his desk. He was talking by speakerphone to William Carter, who had just called to inform him that Alexander Bamus was threatening to withdraw Nibblers' offer if Carter-Crisp didn't accept within 30 days.

"I know what we agreed to last week, but this changes everything," William said.

"No, it doesn't change everything. It doesn't change the fact that Nibblers wants to own our brands and our technology. It doesn't change the fact that most of our people don't want to be part of Nibblers. It doesn't change the fact that Taylor's new product development team is meeting right now in an offsite in Santa Barbara moving heaven and earth to meet the sales and profit targets we gave them. And last, but certainly not least, it doesn't change the fact that your father would never sell this company if there were any way to avoid it and we do have a way to avoid it. Taylor Zobrist and her team will put Carter-Crisp on the innovation pathway again. I guarantee it," Goodrich said, vigorously.

"So what do I tell Alex Bamus?"

"Tell him that we need ninety days to fully consider the impact of selling the company on all of our stakeholder groups—the family, management, employees, distributors, brokers, customers, suppliers, and the other communities we affect."

"He'll say we've already had six months to consider."

"It's taken us six months to warm up to the idea. Now, we need time to seriously consider it. And that means determining whether we can successfully formulate and implement an innovation strategy that will produce the targeted sales and profits within ninety days. If we can make the numbers, then we forego the sale and take the company public in a year or so, when sales and profits are solidly up. If we can't make the numbers, then I'll concede to selling the company."

"What if Bamus doesn't buy it?" William asked.

"He'll buy it. Nibblers has wanted to buy us for years. They're not going to lose interest because of an additional sixty days. Bamus is applying pressure tactics so his department can move on to the next deal. He's just trying to look good for Nibblers' board. Word on the street is he could be the next CEO. He needs this deal."

"Tell me the truth, Nathan. Do you honestly believe Taylor can deliver fifty million dollars in sales and ten million dollars in profits in ninety days?"

"In terms of sales booked with retailers at margins high enough to produce twenty percent in profits, yes, I do. In fact, I think she'll beat it."

"How can you be so sure, when you have so little experience with her?"

"When you've been at this as long as I have, you learn to trust your gut, and my gut tells me she can do this. Which reminds me, we'd be getting a lot more out of Bob Casey right now if the board hadn't rejected his promotion last year."

"You know why we did that; he could never be your replacement and we knew that's where you were headed."

"He's still the most qualified. And now his sagging motivation has become an issue."

"Get rid of him then," William said with a cavalier tone.

William's response bothered Goodrich, but he reminded himself that William wasn't his father. Charlie had understood that talented people needed to be adequately rewarded for their efforts or they'd turn against you—it was a lesson Charlie's son hadn't yet learned. "That's not how we operate around here. You know that."

There was silence on the line for a few moments. Then, William responded, "Maybe that's how you should operate, if you really want to keep the company from being sold. I'll get back to you on the ninety days."

The conversation was over. Both men were cordial as they said good-bye, but Goodrich was irritated with William's immaturity and lack of support.

As soon as Goodrich pressed the speaker button to disconnect from the call, he picked up the receiver and punched in the numbers from the card Taylor had left him. He called her room, but there was no answer. William's call had made him lose track of the time—it was 9:30 P.M. He decided not to leave a message. He'd wait for her to call tomorrow, as they'd planned, after she had two days of the retreat to report on. He would have to tell her about the mounting pressure to sell the company. She deserved to know exactly where things stood.

Goodrich sat down to send Bob Casey a long e-mail asking him to make sure Taylor's new product initiatives got all the necessary support from marketing that they would need. He suggested that Bob come to his office first thing in the morning to discuss marketing's support in detail. He closed his message with an admonishment, "This is a perfect opportunity to show the board that they were wrong about you. See you in the morning."

15

CHAPTER

The second day of the retreat began in the resort's health club with two hours devoted to dance aerobics, muscle strengthening, massage, body scrubs, whirlpool, steam, and sauna. The only requirement for members of the team was to use the time pampering their bodies and preparing their minds for a day of insightful, out-of-the-box thinking (i.e., Perspective Two: Exploit Strategic Advantages). At 10 o'clock everyone gathered under the palm trees on Butterfly Beach to listen to Michael Silva, a well-known consultant with a gift for altering his clients' perceptions by tapping into their inner consciousness. Taylor had worked with Michael a couple of years earlier on a consulting project at Coca-Cola, and she knew he would do a superb job of preparing her team for an intense day of exploiting the competitive advantages in the company's value chain.

Michael began with a story about how eagles learn to fly; young eagles are the most reluctant of all birds to take their first flying leap. Next, he asked the group to pair up and share with each other accounts of the first time they remembered experiencing fear and the first time they remembered experiencing real adversity. Finally, he asked the group to stand up, empty their pockets of any valuables, and follow him into the ocean until the waves were up to their chests.

After listening to the protests and ruling out the possibility of changing their clothes, Michael simply asked them to give up their dread and trust him. The group walked slowly into the foamy surf of the Pacific Ocean—25 abreast through the crashing waves until the 65-degree water just covered the shoulders of Michael's five-foot-two-inch frame. Standing in chest-high waters 30 feet from the sandy beach, the team was invited to spend a few moments reflecting on the experience, and how it related to their first-known fears, their current fears, and the story of how eagles learn to fly.

As Taylor stood in the water, thinking about her fears—the safety of her children, the success of her department, the possibility of more moles in the company, the surveillance, the 90-day deadline, the sale to Nibblers—she admitted to herself that it was easier to overcome her fears when she confronted them head-on. Fear and confidence could not exist in the same person at the same time—one always dominated until it eventually drove out the other. It took confidence to confront fear, which was the first step toward driving it away. She resolved, once again, not to be controlled, manipulated, or hounded by her fears and dreads.

When they finished their reflections they walked, one by one, back to the dry sand of the beach. After obtaining their valuables, they returned to the health club where they removed their wet clothing and put on white sweat pants and shirts with the letters NMDF (No More Dread or Fear) printed on the shirt fronts and pant legs. Then they assembled in the yoga room to wrap up the morning's session.

Using the experience of walking into the cold ocean waves with their clothes on as a metaphor for the dread of discomfort, the fear of adversity, and the reluctance to fly, Michael led the group through an hour of discussion. Later, sharing in pairs further convinced them that altering perspectives—the key to broadening bandwidth and deepening focusdepth—requires breaking through the fears and assumptions that keep people in their comfort zones. As they broke for lunch, Michael left them with a line from Shakespeare: "Love all/ Trust a few/Do wrong to none." His final challenge was to apply Shakespeare's words, not only to people but also to possibilities.

After lunch, the team discussed a multitude of strategic possibilities. The idea of Perspective Two's insightful innovation was to come up with breakthroughs, through a broadened awareness of opportunities and a deepened sense of potential applications, that leveraged the company's existing capabilities into new product categories, customer segments, usage occasions, and channels of distribution.

By late afternoon, to Taylor's delight, everyone was enthusiastically commenting on how productive the brainstorming session had been. In the end, their efforts had identified the following targeted innovations:

Areas of Focus	Innovation Initiatives	Anticipated 90-day	
		Sales	Profits
Product categories	Snack meals	$2m	$0.5m
	Miniature packs	$3m	$0.6m
Customer segments	Kids	$3m	$0.8m
	Natural/organic	$1m	$0.3m
Usage occasions	Breakfast/dinner	Counted above	
Channels	Multilevel marketing	$2m	$0.4m
	Home delivery	$4m	$1m

Before dinner, Taylor called Goodrich as she had promised. She knew he was anxious to hear about the team's progress, and she was excited to tell him everything. Tom had assured her that their conversation would be secure. She reached

Goodrich at the office and gave him an overview of the past 48 hours.

"I'm relieved that you're feeling so positive about the retreat," Goodrich said with a sigh.

The tone in his voice concerned Taylor. "We've still got a long way to go before all of our plans become reality," she said. "But I'm convinced we can make it happen."

"That's what I was hoping you'd say."

It was uncharacteristic for him to be so reticent, Taylor thought to herself. "Is there something I should know?"

Goodrich hesitated. "Nibblers is threatening to withdraw its offer if the company doesn't accept within thirty days. William Carter is getting nervous. I hate to put more pressure on you at a time when the future of the company already seems to be resting on you and your department, but I think you should know exactly where things stand."

"Is the board going to pull the plug on us?" she asked, suddenly dizzy.

"I don't know. They're wrestling with the issue as we speak."

"Is there anything I can do?"

"You're already doing it, Taylor. The only thing that's going to stop the sale of this company is evidence of a revitalized path to growth through innovation. It's the only thing that will convince the family to hold on. If we can convince them that you're going to meet the numbers—and possibly even beat the numbers—we might have a chance."

For Taylor, the words *beat the numbers* sank in deep. The fifty million dollars and ten million dollars were already going to require a Herculean feat. How was she going to *beat* the numbers?

Goodrich continued. "I'll share your progress report with the board, but I'm sure they're going to want to hear it from you early next week."

Taylor asked herself for the thousandth time why she'd accepted this job, but she knew why. It was the perfect opportunity to demonstrate her ability to lead a company through an innovation crisis and onto a path of new growth, and these sorts of career-making opportunities didn't come along everyday. Finally, she said, "We'll be ready, Nathan."

"Thank you, Taylor. Call me when you finish on Friday."

16

CHAPTER

ieter entered the AlphaGraphics Printshop near the Iguatemi Shopping Center and asked for Internet access. His Portuguese was still limited, but fortunately, São Paulo was both English- and Internet-friendly. He logged on, created a new e-mail account through MSN, and composed the following message:

Taylor:
   Someone broke into our apartment and stole all my computer and business files but nothing else. I think it might have been someone from Nibblers trying to find out what I've told you. After you receive and erase this message, I'm changing the e-mail account. If you need to contact me, use this address: emergency2u@hotmail.com. Attached are my recommended contract manufacturers—the for-hire facilities as well as the excess capacity companies I've worked with or thought about working with—and my recommended product innovations—the ones I think have the greatest chance of achieving short-term results. Save the attachments to disc and erase them. This will be my last e-mail, unless you need something else.

Be careful, they may be watching you more closely than you think.

Dieter

Dieter pushed the Send button, but he couldn't help wondering whether he'd just put himself and Taylor in even more danger. The question had plagued him since the break-in. He wanted, even needed, Taylor and Carter-Crisp to succeed, but he also wanted to be well out of it. He and Angela had decided to get married next month in Rio de Janeiro, and he looked forward to moving on with his life.

Dieter left the AlphaGraphics Printshop without noticing the man in a dark suit who had been watching him from across the street. The man was Brazilian and worked for the director of security for Nibblers Latin America.

At 10:00 that evening, Taylor went to the hotel's business center to access the Internet. If there was still no message from Dieter, she'd talk to Tom Platt about it—maybe he'd have some ideas. After logging on and accessing the sedonawaitley@yahoo.com account, she saw the message and opened it. The list of contract manufacturers was long and the recommended innovations included all six of the initiatives identified on the first day of the retreat. She was happy to have Dieter's validation, but the break-in to his apartment was very troubling. Was it possible, she wondered, that someone at Nibblers or Carter-Crisp would go this far to force a deal? She'd read accounts and heard stories about shady, hostile maneuverings when it came to mergers and acquisitions, but this seemed particularly extreme.

Taylor printed the attachments and deleted Dieter's message, but an enormous sense of anxiety rushed over her. Tomorrow would be another crucial day with her team, but it was her children who worried her most suddenly. If these people—these corporate spies, moles, predators—would go to the trouble to track down Dieter in São Paulo, Brazil, and ransack his apartment, what else were they capable of?

Taylor called home. Her mother assured her that everything was fine, the kids were asleep, but something in her voice made Taylor uneasy.

"Don't worry about a thing and get some rest," her mother said. The words comforted her, but she'd still need three Advil to get to sleep. Maybe she was simply missing her children, Taylor told herself. This was the first time she'd been away from home for more than two nights since Jack had died.

17

CHAPTER

hristopher Raia, another guest consultant, kicked off the third day of the retreat (Perspective Three: Develop New Capabilities) by engaging the team with an interactive case study. Over the years, Raia and his partners had developed a wide range of techniques for helping individuals and organizations identify, assess, and develop those new competencies most critical to their future growth. Taylor had used some of his firm's materials with her past clients and knew they could help unleash her team's creative energy at this offsite.

After a brief introduction to the day's interactive process—which would include break-out groups, discussion, decision-making, and creative solution development—Raia projected the opening situation of the case and its first decision point on a large screen in the El Mar conference room. He asked one of the team members to read it out loud to the rest of the group.

You are the new innovation manager for Napoli Spaghetti Sauces and you face some immediate challenges. Napoli, like many of Tuscan Food's big brands, has long been a solid and consistent performer, but growth has slowed in recent years as the trend toward prepared foods and eating out continues to spread across all consumer segments.

One of the primary reasons for Tuscan Food's new focus on fewer, stronger brands is to promote faster growth—Tuscan's parent company has already begun reducing the number of actively managed brands from 800 to a focused portfolio of 200 leading brands. Your challenge is to substantially increase the growth rate of the Napoli brand (currently just under 5 percent annually) within the next 12 months.

The biggest obstacle you face is the shrinking size of the dry goods section, traditionally located in the middle of the store where Napoli Sauces have garnered an impressive reputation and market share. Growth for most grocery stores is coming from the rapidly expanding prepared foods, produce, and meat sections at the outskirts of the store. The middle sections with their dry goods are not only shrinking in terms of allocated shelves, but also in terms of store attention and consumer traffic.

As innovation manager for Napoli Spaghetti Sauces, what would you do to minimize the brand's dependence on grocery store dry goods sections and substantially increase its growth rate? Which options align with which of the four perspectives— Perspective One: Improve Core Businesses; Perspective Two: Exploit Strategic Advantages; Perspective Three: Develop New Capabilities; and Perspective Four: Create Revolutionary Change? Which option would you pursue as your primary focus, and which options would you pursue as your secondary focus?

1. Get to the outskirts of the grocery store by developing a variety of prepared Italian meals and snacks under the Napoli name.

2. Revitalize the Napoli product line with a variety of new specialty sauces and several new convenience packaging

AN INNOVATOR'S TALE

options in order to capture a larger market share from the grocery store dry goods section.

3. Develop a variety of repackaged Napoli products for different channels of distribution, including convenience stores, club stores (e.g., Costco, Sam's Club), fast-food chains, restaurants, and schools.

4. Build direct relationships with consumers through online contact points that include brand-centric sites (e.g., Napoli.com), commerce sites (e.g., major search engines, e-grocers), and needs/solutions sites (e.g., recipe and food preparation sites such as BettyCrocker.com).

5. Break away from your traditional office routine more often, so you can probe more deeply and garner more insights into what consumers really want when it comes to Italian cooking, meals, and sauces.

At the end of the reading, Raia broke the group into five sections, assigned them to break-out rooms with Internet access, provided a few suggested web sites where real-world information could be obtained, and told them they had 30 minutes to make their decisions. Finally, he told them that they would have five minutes to present their group's decisions and rationale at the end of their deliberations.

When the groups returned, they all agreed that option 1 was a Perspective Three innovation, option 2 was Perspective One, option 3 was Perspective Two, option 4 was Perspective Four, and option 5 was all four, depending on the desired level of innovation. However, when it came to choosing a primary and secondary focus, the only thing they could agree on was that all of the options should be pursued simultaneously. It was exactly what Taylor hoped they would conclude.

The rest of the morning unfolded with three more decision-making rounds as the Napoli Spaghetti Sauces case continued with a narrowed focus on Perspective Three's inventive innovation. The ensuing discussions and creative group presentations made Taylor hopeful that the same unbounded imagination, practical creativity, and objective analytical power could be applied to Carter-Crisp's own situation in the afternoon.

After lunch on the veranda with a spectacular view of the gardens and the Santa Ynez Mountains, Taylor's team reconvened in the El Mar conference room to apply Perspective Three innovation to Carter-Crisp. Taylor divided the group into four sections with a different mix of people from the morning's session.

"You've got thirty minutes," she told them, "to decide what new technologies, talents, services, or acquisitions will allow us to increase customer satisfaction and deepen brand or product loyalty. Group one will focus on technologies, group two on talent, group three on services and group four on acquisitions. At the end of thirty minutes, each group will have five minutes to present its ideas and recommendations. We'll shift areas of focus every hour, so each group has the chance to tackle all four areas while building upon the efforts of earlier groups."

There were a few process questions, which Taylor answered before clarifying the afternoon's objective. "Remember, your discussions should focus on technologies, talents, services, or acquisitions that can be developed or purchased within ninety days to produce some level of additional sales and profits. Every recommendation must include a ninety-day sales and profit projection. If you want to identify potential long-term sales and profit projections you may, but that's not our focus during this retreat."

Five hours later, after four rounds of discussions, the team spent another hour finalizing a consolidated Perspective Three innovation plan.

Areas of Focus	Innovation Initiatives	Anticipated 90-Day Sales	Profits
Technologies	Nitrogen packaging	$3m	$0.5m
	Self-heating packs	$5m	$0.9m
Talents	Frozen-food expertise	Counted above	
	Shelf-life expertise	Counted above	
Services	Interactive R&D	$1m	$0.1m
	Snack testing centers	$4m	$0.5m
Acquisitions	Fast-foods companies	$2m	$0.5m
	Catering companies	$2m	$0.4m

Taylor was pleased with the day's results as she went to dinner on the main patio with her team. A quick summary of financial projections from the past three days indicated that they'd already surpassed the targets of $50 million and $10 million in sales and profits given to them by Goodrich and the board. She'd purposely encouraged her team to identify multiple innovation initiatives in each perspective to increase the range of possibilities from which one or more major breakthroughs might emerge—breakthroughs that could generate far more sales and profits than those projected.

Tomorrow, she and her team would have to come up with even more initiative, this time for the next 90 days and beyond. Perspective Four, she told herself, and its look at revolutionary and fundamental change, would be the real key to shaping the long-term future of Carter-Crisp Foods.

18

CHAPTER

lexander Bamus walked into the aristocratic lobby of the Los Angeles Athletic Club where he was greeted by a host and immediately escorted to William Carter's table in the dining room.

"How was your flight?" William said as he stood to shake Alex's hand.

"Not in vain, I hope," Alex returned with a wry smile. He'd returned early from a quick trip to New York City to meet with William.

"You don't waste any time, do you?"

"When you've been courting as long as we have, all you want to hear are the words *I do*." Alex sat down. Tall, classically handsome, and athletic, he was a man who had learned to use his image to his advantage.

"We still need ninety days, Alex."

"As I told you on the phone, I'm not sure we'll still be waiting at the altar in ninety days."

A waiter came to the table and took their orders for lunch.

Alex had already planned his attack: First, hit William hard, then soften him up. "Sorry for the heavy-handedness. We're just anxious. Maybe too anxious. I promise you I'll do everything I can to keep this offer on the table. All I ask in return is an honest answer. Do you really want to do this deal?"

William hesitated. "Yes. But we need the time for due diligence and preparation."

Alex took a sip of wine, thanked William for his candid response, then asked about his son who had just been admitted to Harvard's Kennedy School of Government. William talked a long time about his children. He took his family's position and wealth seriously and had instilled in his children a deep sense of public service. Bamus sensed that William wanted to be done with his father's business so he could devote more time, attention, and resources to community development and cultural education efforts. He served on several prestigious boards—Los Angeles Arts Council, the Getty Museum, board of trustees for the University of Southern California, and the Beverly Hills Chamber of Commerce.

By the time they finished their lunch, Alex and William were talking like old friends. It was the only option Bamus had now, given the circumstances. Casey had been right. It was time for a different kind of pressure. And when the pressure came, Bamus needed to be William's friend, not his adversary.

Before leaving the club, Bamus called Casey to tell him to go ahead with his plans to scare Taylor into leaving the company. When he hung up, he was grateful that he and Casey had agreed to have no electronically traceable contact with each other. If something were to go terribly wrong, he'd be protected.

When Bamus arrived at his Brentwood home, he changed his clothes for a round of golf at the Los Angeles Country Club with the CEO of K&B Foods, another one of Nibbler's current acquisition targets. Alex had already completed two acquisitions since taking the job six months earlier—which had created quite a buzz about him around the executive corridors at Nibblers. If he could close both the K&B and Carter-Crisp deals within the next four months, he'd be a more productive senior VP of mergers and acquisitions than Nibblers' current CEO, Gaspar Ferreira, had been when he held the position 10 years earlier. And it would most certainly put him on the short list of heirs apparent for the top job when Ferreira retired next year.

19

CHAPTER

he last of Taylor's three guest consultants—Don Mangum of Immersion Learning©, a nonprofit organization founded to revolutionize learning systems in all sectors of society—walked to the back of the Loggia Ballroom. He turned down the lights and pushed the button to begin three short video clips. The first was a rapid-fire look at people working, interacting, and traveling throughout the world, accompanied by a deep, authoritative narration:

> Never before in history has the drive for innovation been more inclusive and intense . . . due in large part to the knowledge explosion being fueled by the World Wide Web. A new emerging supercivilization will soon give billions of people the power to interact with one another, to buy and sell goods, create art, organize new business ventures, invent new markets and products, engage in mutually benefiting R&D projects, and learn how to make and distribute everything better, faster, and cheaper . . . than ever before.

The second clip opened inside the kitchen of a busy Manhattan restaurant and proceeded through another rapid-fire series of peeks into dining rooms, fast-food joints, super-markets, shopping malls, and convenience stores where people were eating and shopping. This time, the voice-over was that of an energetic young woman.

> Convenience . . . the mother of all trends. No matter what you think of postmodern society and its countless obsessions, we all seem to crave more conveniences . . . whether it's in the way we receive information, remove waste, transfer funds, travel the world, talk to each other, or feed ourselves . . . we want it to happen faster, easier, better, and cheaper. The drive for convenience is endless.

The third clip began with a view of the earth from outer space, gradually moving closer and closer until it focused in on a small town in the heartland of America and an elementary school with a group of children returning from the playground. The narration started with the voice of a man, then shifted to the voice of a woman, and finally to the voice of a child.

> (*Man's voice*) Learning is accelerated and facilitated when it engages the heart, the mind, and the body . . . forging them into a single powerful force . . . (*Woman's voice*) capable of benefiting fully from individuality, the enlightenment of others and all of God's creations . . . (*Child's voice, as the camera zeros in on the individual children*) I hope I can learn better today.

Don Mangum turned the lights up slightly and placed a graphic of the four innovation perspectives on the screen.

He walked to the front of the room and began describing the four days of the retreat in terms of four different learning dimensions, each dimension corresponding to one of the four perspectives.

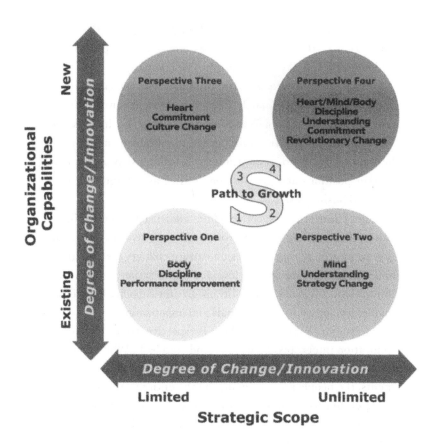

Taylor watched the members of her team for their reactions. All eyes were glued to Mangum as he spoke. She still had some lingering reservations about the day's agenda, but even if it didn't work as well as she'd hoped, the past three days had been extremely successful. She listened as Mangum spoke.

On Tuesday, Perspective One was about incremental innovation that comes primarily from the body, involves adding new discipline, and focuses on performance improvement. Just as nutrition and exercise bring health and strength to the body, innovation in this dimension brings continuous improvement and higher levels of performance to the company.

On Wednesday, Perspective Two dealt with insightful innovation that comes primarily from the mind, involves gaining new understanding, and focuses on strategy change. In the same way reading and studying bring greater knowledge and comprehension to the mind, innovation in this dimension brings new market positions and greater competitive advantages to products and businesses.

On Thursday, Perspective Three addressed inventive innovation that comes primarily from the heart, involves acquiring new commitment, and focuses on culture change. Just as caring and nurturing bring greater love and appreciation to the heart, innovation in this dimension brings greater capacity for growth and to development to individuals and organizations.

Today you'll experience how Perspective Four's ingenious innovation integrates the heart, mind, and body. When they are united in purpose, individuals can transform their environments, the people around them, and the entire world. The same thing occurs when innovation in this dimension combines the powers of the body, mind, and heart to create a bold new future through revolutionary change.

Mangum answered a few questions and then surprised everyone, except Taylor who knew what was coming. He told the group that they'd be dividing into five groups to make video documentaries of Carter-Crisp's future. After the laughs and jokes subsided, he assured them that he was serious and that there were five video software technicians waiting in each of the break-out rooms to provide access to the necessary resources: a library of stock film footage, music, scripting and storyboarding software, and a variety of other desktop movie-making tools.

Referring to the three earlier video clips as examples, Mangum charged each of the break-out teams to create a 10-minute video capturing a revolutionary vision of the future, a future that could begin within 90 days. New business models, new industries, new markets, and new organizations were all fair game. The strategic possibilities were unlimited and if the needed capabilities existed somewhere in the world, they could be acquired.

Each group would have four hours to develop its own video. One person in each group would be asked to monitor heart involvement, another person would be assigned to monitor mind involvement, a third appointed to monitor body involvement, and a fourth appointed to monitor the combination of body, mind, and heart to ensure that all four sources of innovation—discipline, understanding, commitment, and their union—were being actively engaged by every member of the group.

Four hours later, the groups presented their video productions with incredible results. The entire process was the most creative treatment of a company's future that Taylor had ever experienced.

One group portrayed the company's revolutionary future as home delivery of snack foods and proposed to implement it immediately through the acquisition of a major pizza delivery company. Another group envisioned an alliance with a major online bookseller in order to sell snacks online. Yet another group presented a scenario that involved setting up snack food testing centers inside large grocery stores. The fourth group projected a revolutionary way of involving customers in the snack food research and development process by allowing them to participate in experiments and research online with free samples delivered by UPS. The last group presented a radically expanded range of snack foods with Italian, Asian, French, Mid-East, and Brazilian groupings based on new applications of pasta, rice, fruit, and internationally famous sauces.

The video presentations were stunning, and easily the peak experience of the entire week. It turned out to be the perfect way to end the planning phase and begin the implementation phase. Another $30 million in sales and $6 million in profits that could be generated in 90 days had been identified in Perspective Four, but, of course, not all of these radical innovations could be implemented simultaneously—unless Taylor and her team figured out a way to combine some of them. Even then, it would take a major commitment on the part of the board to make the necessary investment, acquisitions, and alliances.

As Taylor and her key managers went to a final dinner Friday night in the nearby Danish village of Solvang, she felt, more than ever, that they had mapped out a path to growth through innovation that could keep Carter-Crisp Foods from being sold. The feeling was absolutely exhilarating.

20
CHAPTER

L ate Friday afternoon, as Taylor's team was beginning its video presentations in Santa Barbara, her children were getting off the school bus near their condominium in Marina del Rey. Kate walked with two other girls several feet ahead of her brother and his friend Matt. As the children got closer to home—most of them lived in the same condominium complex as Kate and Jeremy—they walked past the marina and the docks.

Jeremy and Matt watched eagerly as the weekend sailors prepared their vessels. Both boys loved to sail and each hoped for a small boat of his own on which he could perfect his sailing skills. They stopped to watch the preparations on one of the 40-footers, a beautiful yacht with a mast that soared 50 feet into the air, clearly the tallest in the harbor.

When Kate looked back and saw that Jeremy and Matt had stopped, she yelled at her brother. "Jeremy, come on. Grandma's waiting for us. Remember what Mom said."

"I'm coming," Jeremy yelled.

A man emerged from the cabin of the 40-footer and looked at Jeremy and Matt who were still standing on the dock watching.

"You boys want to take a closer look?" he asked.

Jeremy and Matt glanced at each other, then at Kate who was walking again, and then at the man. There were two other people on the deck—a boy and girl in their late teens or early twenties. "How unsafe could it be?" Jeremy asked himself. His mother had scared him to death about talking to strangers, especially men, but this man was a neighbor and those were probably his own kids.

"Sure," Jeremy said. He shrugged and looked at Matt whose face was bright with excitement.

The man walked to the gate on the main pier and let the boys board his boat. Jeremy and Matt had been on lots of sailboats before, but not one this big.

"What are your names?" the man asked as he watched the boys look around.

With some hesitation, Jeremy spoke. "I'm Jeremy Zobrist and this is Matt Calle. We live over there," he said, pointing to the condominium tower 200 feet away.

"Ever been on a boat this big?"

"Uhh, no," Jeremy said as he and Matt walked over to the mast and touched it.

The man explained how the sails could be released for maximum speed on the open ocean.

"Do you race?" Jeremy asked. Racing in the America's Cup competition was a dream that he and Matt shared.

The man leaned against the deck's railing and smiled broadly. "Close-quarter racing in choppy seas exposes the real strength and stamina of a championship crew. It's like no other feeling in the world."

"Awesome," Matt said.

"Would you like to take a look downstairs?" the man asked as he walked toward the open cabin door. The boys followed.

Inside the opulent cabin, he gave them a tour and a couple of cokes from the maple wood–covered refrigerator. As

Jeremy and Matt gulped down their sodas and admired their surroundings, Jeremy heard his sister yelling his name.

"Thanks, but we gotta go now."

"Why don't you talk to your mother about coming for a sail?"

"You know my mother?" Jeremy asked, surprised.

"Taylor Zobrist, right?"

"Yeah. Do you live in the condos?"

"No, but I work in the same business."

"You work for Carter-Crisp?" Jeremy asked.

"I work for Nibblers, a competitor of Carter-Crisp's."

Then the man came closer to the two boys and put his hands on their shoulders. "Come back anytime and don't forget to ask your parents if you can come sailing with us."

As the boys turned to climb the stairs, the man moved his hand to Jeremy's neck, tousling the back of his hair. It made Jeremy feel uncomfortable and he hurried to get out of the cabin.

"Jeremy. What are you doing?" Kate screamed as she came running down the pier.

"We were just taking a look."

"Come on, right now."

The boys walked quickly down the plank to the dock and through the gate.

After receiving a good scolding from Kate, which Jeremy quickly brushed aside with a flick of his hand, he looked back at the boat. The man was on the deck and waved to him.

21

CHAPTER

aturday morning while making breakfast and catching up on her children's activities, Taylor asked about what had happened during the week. She saw Kate and Jeremy exchange glances.

"What's going on?" she asked. "Is there something you need to tell me, Jeremy? Kate?"

"Matt and I went onto a man's sailboat in the marina, but it was no big deal," Jeremy said with a flippant air. "His kids were with him. Plus, he said he knew you."

"What's his name?" Taylor asked, feeling a pinch of unease. She had told her children, again and again, not to talk to strangers and certainly not to be drawn in by them even if the allure was a sailboat, something her son loved.

"I don't know his name, but his boat's got the tallest mast in the marina," Jeremy told her. He reached for another muffin.

"He said he worked for Nibblers," Kate added with an air of sibling superiority.

Taylor's body tensed. "Tell me exactly what he said." She saw Jeremy's face take on a worried look; he thought she was angry at him. But she was more scared than angry.

"He said you worked together," Jeremy said. "So I thought he meant he worked at Carter-Crisp. But he said he worked for Nibblers. That's all."

"That's it?"

"He told us to ask our parents if we could go sailing with him." Jeremy looked down at his plate.

"What is it?" Taylor urged. "Tell me."

"The way he put his hand on my shoulder and messed up my hair made me feel weird. I'm sorry, Mom."

Taylor walked over to her son and soothed him as he began to cry, assuring him that everything would be okay.

She knew that the one thing she was supposed to do— protect her children—she'd failed at. She'd let them and the memory of their father down. No job was worth it. Sadness soon turned into anger at herself for getting them into this situation, and whoever it was at Nibblers or Carter-Crisp responsible for this. How far would these people go? Would they stop at nothing to get what they wanted?

Later, the three of them walked down to the marina where the sailboat had been. The 40-foot sailing yacht was gone, and even more troubling, there was no record of any boat mooring in that particular slip during the past 36 hours. The last boat to rent the slip had left two days earlier. Only one person in the marina office remembered seeing a tall-masted sailboat, and she hadn't paid much attention.

When Taylor and her children got home, she immediately called Tom Platt and told him the story. He instructed her to call the police and then suggested that her children be placed under protective surveillance. Taylor agreed. She called the Marina del Rey police and reported the incident to the watch commander. Unfortunately, neither Jeremy nor Kate could remember any of the numbers or names on the sailboat.

When Taylor explained that the incident might have something to do with Nibblers attempt to buy Carter-Crisp, the commander's response was cool. He told her she would have to produce evidence for any investigation to be undertaken.

For the rest of the weekend, Taylor agonized over the situation. Should she resign in order to protect her children or should she rely on Tom Platt and the police to protect them while she did everything she could to keep Carter-Crisp from being sold to Nibblers and find the people who were doing this? By Sunday night, Taylor had made her decision: She would resign. Nothing was worth putting her children in jeopardy.

Only two days earlier, Taylor had assured Goodrich that Carter-Crisp would be able to meet and possibly surpass the targeted numbers. Now she would have to give him her resignation and tell him everything Dieter had told her about Nibblers. It didn't matter any more who was or wasn't part of Nibblers' scheme. She would give Goodrich two weeks' notice and be gone, out of this mess, and there was nothing he or Tom Platt could say or do that was going to change her mind.

22

CHAPTER

*M*onday morning the new products area on the second floor of the Carter-Crisp building was bustling with activity and contagious enthusiasm. All who had attended the retreat were playfully referring to the experience as "The Santa Barbara Mission," and "Four Days That Changed the Snack Food World." Without exception, they were functioning at a new level of energy with a deeper common purpose, and the entire area buzzed with excitement.

When Taylor arrived at her office a little later than usual, she struggled to hide her mood. She did not want it to detract from the palpable energy. She told Amy Grow to screen all calls and interruptions for the next hour and 15 minutes so she could prepare for her 10:30 meeting with Goodrich. She went into her office and closed the door; not the best attitude, she knew, on this first day back after the retreat.

She knew she should be out there cheerleading the effort and reinforcing the common purpose, especially when every single day of implementation was so critical. But everything had changed since Jeremy told her what happened at the marina. She wondered who her predators would target next, after she was gone. She had to convince Goodrich that the threat was real. After that it would be his problem to solve. The thought made her ache inside. If she were Goodrich's age, if her children were grown, maybe she'd stay and fight. The thought brought her little comfort.

Taylor sat down to summarize the results of the retreat and document the path of implementation. The first three days had produced projected sales and profits of $54 million and $11.1 million, respectively. She expected only about 70 percent of those projections to be actually realized, which translated to $38 million in sales and $8 million in profits. That meant at least $12 million in sales and $2 million in profits had to come from Perspective Four, which produced sales and profits projections of $30 million and $6 million. As she went over the summary, she felt comfortable that the targeted $50 million and $10 million could be met and maybe surpassed—if an aggressive implementation plan could be successfully executed. But all of it would depend on who replaced her. Carter-Crisp would have to deal with Nibblers without her—even though criminal means were being used to force the sale of the company. After the acquisition, she thought to herself, most of the Carter-Crisp employees would probably leave over time, if they weren't fired. There were worse things, she knew.

As Taylor began charting out the critical milestones for implementing each of the innovations identified during the retreat, Amy opened the door and handed Taylor a FedEx letter.

"There are several people who want to talk with you after your meeting with Goodrich. Should I tell them that you'll be available this afternoon?" Amy asked.

"Actually, I'd like to have a staff meeting at two o'clock with everyone who attended the retreat. Can you arrange for one of the conference rooms?"

Amy said she'd take care of it and closed the door behind her. The FedEx letter was from David Cross of Cross Associates. The name wasn't familiar to her. Although apprehensive, she opened it and withdrew a single-page letter on Cross Associates letterhead, but there was no address or phone number, just a row of cities—New York, San Francisco, Tokyo, Paris, Milan, and Buenos Aires.

Dear Taylor:

I am the man who invited your son Jeremy onto my sailing yacht last Friday. He's a delightful boy. My purpose in writing you is to explain that I am only an intermediary paid to deliver a message.

- Do not allow Carter-Crisp Foods to obtain more than $25 million in sales and $5 million in profits from new products and other innovations during the next 90 days.

- Do not have any further contact with the police or any other law enforcement agency. If they contact you, do not give them any additional information.

- Do not discuss any of this with anyone, including Dieter Wilkins.

- Do not resign from the company.

- Terminate the services of Tom Platt.

- Destroy this letter once you have read it.

If you meet these demands, you and your children and Dieter and his girlfriend will remain safe and untouched. But if you do not, you will put yourself and them in jeopardy. When the 90 days are over, you may do whatever you wish, as long as you do not talk about any of this. If you choose to remain with the company under the new ownership, you will receive ample resources and incentives to implement all of the innovations you and your team identified during your Santa Barbara retreat.

Sincerely,
David D. Cross

This can't be happening, Taylor told herself, as she read the letter again. Are these people insane? How far will they really go? Again and again, she asked herself these questions, but couldn't answer them. Her feelings of powerlessness and helplessness were overwhelming.

Tears filled her eyes as she thought about Jeremy and Kate, and what she'd gotten them into so stupidly. She quickly folded the letter and stuffed it into her purse, then she took a sheet of letterhead from her desk and walked to the paper shredder located outside her office. She folded the blank sheet of letterhead and fed it into the machine, just in case someone was watching. Whether she believed the threat was real or not didn't matter, she realized. She had to assume it was.

Taylor returned to her desk in quiet anguish and waited. She was dying inside but couldn't let it show. No matter how much she wanted to tell Goodrich about what was happening, she couldn't. She wouldn't. If she did, they'd find out. Whoever *they* were.

23

CHAPTER

athan Goodrich went looking for Taylor when she hadn't shown up at his office by 10:40. He told himself a trip down to the second floor would give him the opportunity to personally congratulate the people in new products for their work at the retreat. As he made his way through the maze of offices and cubicles, shaking hands and spreading words of encouragement, Goodrich couldn't help but notice the high energy levels and sense of optimism among the people in the department. He was pleased and feeling more and more relieved all the time.

When he arrived at Taylor's office, he found her door shut. Amy Grow shrugged and said, "I told her she was late and that was twenty minutes ago. I think she's still working on something for you."

Goodrich knocked. "You ready for me?" he asked, as he stepped inside.

Taylor turned from the window behind her desk and quickly stood. "I'm sorry, I lost track of time. Sit down," she said, gesturing to the chairs around the small conference table in the corner of the room. She gathered the stack of papers from her desk and sat down next to her boss.

Goodrich sensed Taylor's distraction but assumed it was preoccupation with the enormous task at hand. "You're not overdoing it, are you? I know we've put a lot of pressure on you, but we don't want to drive you out of the company." His words made her gasp.

"I'll be fine," she said, "but meeting the targets isn't going to be easy."

"Having any second thoughts?" he asked, studying her closely.

"No, it's just that we've got our work cut out for us," she said.

Goodrich leaned forward. "Do you really think we can make it?"

"Yes, Nathan. I think we can make it, if everything falls into place and you can provide the necessary resources."

"I told you on Friday, you'll have all the resources you need," Goodrich said, trying to reassure her.

For the next 10 minutes, Taylor reviewed with Goodrich a summary of the retreat and her detailed implementation plan. The more they talked, the more comfortable he felt, but he was concerned about the strain he saw on her face and the hesitation in her voice. Was she pushing herself too hard? Was she in over her head? Or was there some other reason for her tentativeness? Whatever it was, he needed to help her overcome it. She was the company's final hope.

Alone, Taylor cried. She wasn't sure why, but her doubts about Goodrich—the ones she'd discarded soon after accepting her new assignment—had come flooding back, only this time stronger. Her head was spinning with questions: Did Goodrich know what was going on? Was he being threatened, too? Was he part of the scheme? Was he the one pulling the strings? She didn't know, and probably never would. But she really didn't care at the moment. Right now, all she wanted was for Nibblers to acquire Carter-Crisp, and then she could quit.

As soon as the thought crossed her mind, she considered the horrible possibility that they'd never leave her alone. Then her thoughts about Goodrich deepened. The concerned eyes, the wrinkled brow, the on-edge posture, the tone of voice— they all suggested to Taylor that he *wasn't* involved. Again, her intuition told her he could never be involved in a secret plot to sell the company to Nibblers. The realization pained her because there was no way she could think of to protect her children and Dieter and Angela, and at the same time, save the company from Nibblers' clutches.

It was as if she were being torn in half. She had to get out of the office for a couple hours to regain her composure and told Amy she'd be back for the two o'clock staff meeting.

On her way out, she ran into Bob Casey, VP of marketing. "I hear your retreat was a great success," he said as they passed in the corridor. "Let's have lunch this week so you can bring me up to speed."

Taylor didn't want to stop and talk. Her only hope was to keep walking. "Let me check my schedule and I'll get back to you," she said.

"I'll be waiting," he said, smiling.

Taylor had heard stories about his womanizing; the man was too good-looking for his own good. Then she wondered, is he the one? It was possible. She'd never felt comfortable around him, and there was something menacing about him. But was she out of control now? Would she suspect everyone who spoke to her or gave her a smile?

Twenty minutes later, Taylor was barefoot and walking on the wet sand of Santa Monica beach. Sadly, the ocean's surf didn't have its usual calming influence on her. Someone called her name from behind.

Startled, she turned around. It was Tom Platt who had followed her when she left the office.

"What happened?" he asked.

"Nothing. I just needed to clear my head."

"If you don't tell me the truth, I can't help you," Tom returned. "Look at you. What's wrong? Tell me."

"I can't," she said.

Tom reached out awkwardly, but she stepped back and turned away from him. Even Tom couldn't help her now, she thought.

"If you give in to their demands now, they'll never leave you alone," he said.

"You know?" she blurted out as she turned around.

"We know that you received something in a FedEx package that upset you. Our assumption is that it was a threat."

Taylor looked around her. "They're probably watching us right now," she said as she began trudging through the dry sand toward her car. "They're watching me with *you*."

"I doubt it," Tom said. He didn't move from his spot on the beach.

"How can you be so sure?" she asked angrily.

"First, no one followed you. Second, they're counting on their threat to scare you into quitting. Third, if you don't scare easily, they'll threaten you again before they take any other action. Fourth, they know I'm still on the job, so they won't attempt to track or monitor you as long as I'm around. They probably told you to get rid of me, right?"

They walked the beach for the next 30 minutes as Taylor showed him the letter from David Cross of Cross Associates and agonized over her dilemma. By the time they returned to her car, she had agreed to let Tom prepare a plan for protecting her family and Dieter Wilkins.

"If I'm not convinced by your plan I won't follow it," Taylor said, opening the door of her car.

"That's fine. But remember, you'll never be rid of them. Not when you know what you know."

"And you need to remember that it's not your decision. It's mine."

"Trust your intuition, Taylor. You can't let them get away with this. Do what you'd do if you only had to worry about yourself. Let me worry about protecting your family." Tom held the car door open. "In the meantime, I suggest you warn Dieter."

On her way back to the office, Taylor stopped at a Kinko's to send an e-mail to Dieter via the emergency address that he'd given her. Her hands were shaking so hard, she had to hold herself steady for a few minutes before typing in her message of warning and sending it.

24

CHAPTER

uring his lunch break, Dieter checked the emergency e-mail account from a public-access Internet kiosk in the business center of the Omni Hotel. There was a message from Taylor:

> Dieter:
>
> Whoever's behind this made contact with my children as a way of scaring me. They did a good job of it. They also threatened to take action against you and Angela if I don't do as they say. My security consultant Tom Platt and I both thought you should know about the threats. Tom thinks someone from Nibblers or Carter-Crisp ransacked your apartment and took your files and computer. He thinks you're being followed. I'll let you know what we decide to do on this end.
>
> Be careful,
> Taylor

As soon as Dieter read the message, he left the hotel for his office on Avenida Paulista. He took the elevator to the 15th floor, walked into his suite, and closed the door behind him. It was all too much. They'd gone too far. He was not about to put Angela or himself in danger. And what about Taylor and her children?

By the time he left his office three hours later, he'd made a decision. Tomorrow, he would tell his boss that he needed to take a three-month leave of absence for personal reasons. His boss would probably tell him that he was crazy and that no company in its right mind would accommodate such a request from an employee who'd been on the job for less than a month. Dieter would have to agree, and then he'd resign. It was that simple. He and Angela had to disappear for a while.

She wouldn't be happy about postponing the wedding, he knew, but the idea of spending more time together would appeal to her. The break-in had rattled her, and she was more than ready to move. With their combined financial resources they could live for a while, maybe two or three years, without working. Now, all he had to do was figure out how to lose his surveillants. He looked around him several times as he climbed into his car and drove out of the parking garage onto the busy Avenida.

25

CHAPTER

om Platt looked at the list of summer resorts he'd written down on a legal pad. Of the ten listed, there were only three he hadn't crossed out: Dana Place, New Hampshire; Jackson Hole, Wyoming; and Vail, Colorado. After another 30 minutes on the Internet, he crossed out two more—Dana Place and Vail. That left only Jackson Hole. He immediately called his surveillance team and asked them to prepare a full report on the summer activities available in Jackson Hole for grandmothers and grandchildren, ages 9 and 11.

Within two hours, Tom had a complete file of materials. There were classes on horseback riding, art, photography, sailing on Yellowstone Lake, writing and literature, fishing, nature workshops, mountain climbing, river rafting, and horticulture. It would be a perfect, isolated summer environment for Jeremy and Kate Zobrist and their grandmother, Eileen Stansbury. More important, Tom was convinced that he could keep them secure at a place called High Teton Ranch.

When Tom arrived at Taylor's office, he gave her his recommmendation. "School ends in three weeks. The people who've threatened you will be expecting you to attempt a relocation for the summer. I suggest you move your family at the end of this week. They can finish their schoolwork in Jackson." Tom sat in one of the leather chairs in front of Taylor's desk.

"They'll be devastated, having to miss the last two weeks of school."

"It's the best way to ensure a safe exit."

"Safe exit? You make it sound so ominous."

"I don't mean to be overly dramatic, but these are extreme and unusual measures. If we could bring in the FBI without increasing the danger to you and your family, we would," Tom said. "I want to make sure you understand our top priority is to protect your children and your mother."

"Can I visit them?"

"Of course. We'll just have to make sure that no one follows you, but that shouldn't be a problem."

"Are you sure you can keep them safe?" Taylor hesitated. "What if something goes wrong?"

"No course of action is without risk, Taylor," Tom said, his voice calm yet commanding. "But, we have a much better chance of keeping your family safe in Jackson than we do in Los Angeles."

"What do we do when they find out that I've sent them away for the summer?" Taylor asked. "They'll know if they're watching me."

"Just make sure you keep sales and profits below their ceilings until we discover who they are," Tom instructed. "Which means you'll have to find a creative way to hide the numbers until the last minute."

"That won't be easy when we don't have any idea who we're trying to hide them from." She sighed heavily.

"I'm working on it," Tom said.

"Do you have new information?" Taylor asked, excitedly. If Tom could, even tentatively, identify the possible moles who were feeding information to Nibblers, maybe she could keep them out of the information loop.

"I don't think Goodrich is involved," Tom said. "We've done a thorough background check on him and there's nothing—no pattern, no motive, no reason—to suggest that he would ever consider selling out Carter-Crisp Foods. Charlie Carter handpicked Goodrich because of his loyalty and integrity, and the man has delivered consistently over the years. Of the other senior executives, only Bob Casey seems to have a motive for selling out. He was passed over for a promotion last year and he was not happy about it. He also seems to live somewhat of a double life—polished business professional and corporate marketer during the day, womanizer and barhopper at night. And he knows Alexander Bamus from Nibblers."

Taylor's face dropped. "Isn't he the one negotiating with the board?"

Tom nodded. "He's Nibblers' Senior VP of Mergers and Acquisitions."

"How do they know each other?"

"Officially, they don't. But they've been seen together at a place called Baci's in Westwood. For what it's worth, Casey's the only one on our radar screen right now. But we're still investigating others. We're also delving deeper into William Carter's background and relationships. He's the one putting the most pressure on Goodrich to sell the company."

"What you're telling me is that I should give Casey nothing."

"Yes."

"That won't be easy, because he's responsible for marketing everything we develop," Taylor said in frustration.

"I think it's time you start thinking in terms of a plan B," Tom said. "Can I tell my people to go ahead with their preparations for Jackson Hole?"

117

Taylor looked at him. Part of her liked his direct manner, his decisiveness, and the way he made her feel as competent and capable in her field as he was in his. However, part of her was put off by his brisk style, abrupt approach, and risk-taking attitude. Still, as things stood, she had no one else to turn to, no one else to trust, and she did appreciate his concern for her family.

"When do I need to have them ready?" she finally asked.

"We'll pick them up early Sunday morning. I'll give you the details tomorrow."

"By the way, they expect me to fire you."

"I know. We're setting up shop in one of the first-floor condos in your building. From now on, you'll need to contact me from home, unless it's an emergency. My people will continue monitoring this building and your condo, but they'll be doing it at arm's length. In other words, they won't be seen or heard. As far as Carter-Crisp and any of its shareholders or employees are concerned, our services will be terminated as of right now. You should have accounts payable cut us a check immediately."

There was so much to be uncertain about. "Will this situation *ever* be resolved?" she asked.

"You worry about beating the numbers and keeping it a secret from Casey and the rest of the company, I'll worry about exposing the conspirators. And yes, the situation will be resolved—without harm to you or your family."

"Dieter and Angela, too?"

Tom hesitated uncharacteristically. He spoke slowly and deliberately. "Dieter and his girlfriend are out of scope. We don't have the resources to protect someone in South America."

"What do you mean *out of scope?*"

"You warned him. Now we have to assume he'll take the necessary steps to protect himself."

"But I'm making a choice that puts him in harm's way," Taylor said, struck by Tom's indifference.

"We're aware of that. What would you like us to do?"

"Protect him."

"Don't misinterpret this, but it will cost more than we agreed to."

"I don't care what it costs," she said angrily. "This is his life!"

Taylor watched with mixed feelings as Tom left her office. She was immensely grateful to have him on her side—he had given her new hope that she could both protect her children and keep the company from being consumed by Nibblers— but she still wondered about his cool detachment. Jack used to get that way at times, and she had never liked it when he did. What concerned her most, however, was her growing dependence on Tom and her increasing willingness to follow his lead. Nevertheless, she felt that she was doing the right thing.

26

CHAPTER

At 4:00 A.M., Sunday morning, Tom Platt called Taylor to inform her that he was ready to take her family to the airport. Ten minutes later, in the darkness of the building's parking garage, Taylor, Kate, Jeremy, and Taylor's mother Eileen entered the white panel van while Tom and two other men loaded the luggage. When the van left the garage, Taylor thought it looked like workers leaving for a weekend job.

Thirty-six hours later, after getting her family settled at the High Teton Ranch just outside Jackson Hole, Wyoming, Taylor hugged her children and mother, and told them she would see them in a couple of weeks. Leaving to go back to Carter-Crisp was one of the hardest things she'd ever done, but she had reconciled herself to it. Tom was the last one she hugged.

"Take care of them," she whispered in Tom's ear. "I couldn't do this if I didn't trust you completely." She hoped he knew how much his confident reassurances meant to her.

"Don't worry, my people won't let them out of their sight," Tom said. He told Taylor he had assigned his two best man-woman teams and a high-tech surveillance expert to watch over her family. But both he and Taylor understood that the longer it took to find the mole inside Carter-Crisp, the riskier the situation would become for all of them. "I'll be back in LA by the end of the week, but you know what to do if you need to contact me."

Taylor nodded and got into the SUV that would return her to Jackson Hole's airport. She gave a final appreciative glance at Tom as the car drove away. He had promised to stay a few days with her family to make sure everything was safe, secure, and tranquil, and she was grateful.

On the long flight back to Los Angeles, Taylor struggled with her emotions and the rising resentment she felt toward those who had put her in this intolerable position. Slowly but surely, her feelings of victimization turned to determination. Tom had been right, now that her children were safe and sequestered, she was ready to fight—and fight hard.

By the time the Gulfstream V rolled up to the executive terminal at LAX, Taylor had formulated a plan to radically reorganize her department around the four perspectives from the retreat. The plan was to focus two of her most practical and detail-oriented directors and seven managers on Perspective One, implementing the six product extension and improvement initiatives that projected sales and profits of $22 million and $4.6 million. Her other three directors and 12 managers would be assigned to Perspectives Two, Three, and Four—with combined projected sales and profits of $62 million and $12.5 million. For Perspective Two, she'd need her most strategically gifted director and managers to exploit the company's competitive advantages in new ways. Perspective Three would require her most corporate culture–sensitive and technology-oriented director and managers to develop and acquire the new capabilities necessary to increase customer satisfaction and brand loyalty. Finally, Perspective Four would demand her most creative and unorthodox director and managers to realize the revolutionary ideas developed at the retreat.

After the same white panel van that had taken her to the airport returned her to her now empty condo, she spent the rest of the evening drawing organizational charts and placing the names of her people in boxes. Immersing herself in the work of restructuring her department not only kept her focused but also allowed her to think more creatively and strategically. It wouldn't be enough, she realized, to reorganize along the four different perspectives; she would also have to physically relocate her people in Perspectives Two, Three, and Four, because everything outside of the work in Perspective One would have to be hidden from the rest of the organization. And she'd have to do it without raising suspicion. This meant that R&D, market testing, manufacturing, distribution, marketing, and sales would all have to be outsourced. It wouldn't be easy and it wouldn't be cheap, but Taylor was convinced that it was the safest course of action.

First thing in the morning, she'd go to Kinko's in the mall and e-mail Dieter. His list of manufacturing contractors was invaluable, and she hoped he'd be able to provide the same sort of input on contractors that could provide R&D, marketing, distribution, and sales services. Then, she'd request an emergency meeting with Goodrich to let him know about the funding she'd need to establish a divergent organization outside Carter-Crisp. Her argument would be that Carter-Crisp would have its hands full with implementing the initiatives from Perspective One, and she didn't want the initiatives from the other three perspectives to distract or overwhelm. Then she'd tell him she

wanted to keep everything related to the divergent organization a secret for as long as possible.

It would be a tough sell and an even tougher execution,
but she was now in full fighting form. One way or another,
she and Tom were going to beat, and then expose, the predators who'd put her in this situation.

27
CHAPTER

ieter and Angela had just finished an early-morning walk on the beach at Guarujá near Hotel Casa Grande where they were staying for a few days. They'd placed Angela's condo on the market, stored their belongings, and embarked on a trip up the Brazilian coastline in search of beautiful beaches, great hotels with romantic settings, and safety. Angela was ecstatic and Dieter was relieved. The only thing that bothered him was the situation back at Carter-Crisp Foods. His feelings of guilt about Taylor Zobrist and her situation were increasing.

Once back at the hotel, Angela went to the spa for a salt rub while Dieter went to the business center to check e-mail. He logged on and checked the emergency account but there was nothing. He then checked another temporary account he'd set up to receive e-mails from Kibon.

The agreement he'd struck with his new employer was to provide approximately 10 hours of consulting per week for three months until he could resume his full-time duties. It was a generous arrangement for which Dieter had promised to stay in touch through e-mail on a daily basis. As he was finishing his reply to one of his subordinates at Kibon, he heard the familiar "ping," announcing an incoming message—it was on the emergency account—but nothing showed up on the screen. He quickly sent a message to Taylor.

Taylor:
    Just receiving your e-mail. Give me a minute and I'll respond.

Dieter

After sending the message in hope that Taylor would get it before logging off, Taylor's message appeared on the screen. He was anxious to find out what she'd decided to do, since it could have a big impact on his and Angela's future as well as his peace of mind; Carter-Crisp was a company he'd helped build over the past 10 years. If she decided to give in to the conspirators, it would make life easier for him. If she decided to fight, however, it would be better for everyone in the long run, even though the next few months would be dangerous. Fighting was something he could never have done, but Taylor was stronger than he was. He felt embarrassed to admit it, but it was true. He read her message.

Dieter:
    I've decided to stay and fight. It wasn't an easy decision and I know it has serious implications for you and Angela. I have arranged for Tom Platt's organization to provide protection for both of you. I'm reorganizing the department. Anything more radical than product extension and improvement will be hidden in a divergent operation and outsourced—manufacturing, distribution, marketing, and sales, even the brand names will be new. It will make our task of meeting the $50 million and $10 million targets more difficult in the beginning, but as we get going it will make things much simpler and more streamlined.

Platt thinks Bob Casey may be involved with Nibblers, but he can't say for sure yet, so we plan to keep everybody except Goodrich in the dark. I could use your help identifying additional independent contractors and consultants for R&D, marketing, distribution, and sales. We're already using your list of manufacturing contractors, and your recommended product innovations served as a good confirmation for our recent retreat. Let me know as soon as possible how you'd like to make contact with Tom Platt. He's great, and I trust him completely.

Taylor

Dieter was grateful for Taylor's resolve. He vowed, as he typed his response, to help her in any way possible—it was the least he could do.

Taylor:

First, I think you've made the right decision, and I'm sure it wasn't easy. Second, there's no need for Platt to worry about us. We've left São Paulo and will be traveling for the next three months. We won't be using any credit cards or making any phone calls. The only contact I'll have with my company is through a special e-mail account, but it's outside the company's normal system. We also went to great lengths to make sure no one followed us when we left São Paulo. Just take care of yourself and your family. Third, I don't have the benefit of my files, but I can use the Internet to get you a pretty good list of additional contractors and consultants in a few days. Finally, as much as I hate to admit it, I think Platt may be right about Casey. He never got over having his promotion denied, and he and Chimura were always very chummy. If he's involved, there could be others because he has a strong and loyal following inside the company. I'll plan to change the emergency e-mail account on a weekly basis just to be safe.

Dieter

Within a few minutes, Dieter received another message from Taylor.

> Glad to know you're safe. Please be careful. If you need Tom Platt's protection, I'll make sure his people are ready to respond immediately. At a minimum, you should consider having him set up a contingency plan for you and Angela, in case you need to change locations quickly. Mine will reunite me with my children within three hours. Think about it. In the meantime, get me your list of contractors and consultants as soon as you can, and let me know if you remember anything else strange or unusual about Casey or any of his people. I'll be in touch.
>
> Taylor

Dieter logged off the computer, paid his bill in cash, and walked briskly out of the business center toward his hotel room. He was happy that his input had helped Taylor, it helped ease his conscience, but he was still worried about her. She'd obviously had to relocate her children because of the threats, and the thought made him cringe inside. She didn't deserve what she was going through, but there was nothing else he could do—at least, that's what he told himself.

28
CHAPTER

"She's still e-mailing somebody from Kinko's," Derek Jamison said after entering Casey's office and closing the door behind him. "And her children are gone."

"Can she be that stupid?" Casey stood up from his leather executive chair and began pacing between his desk and wall-length credenza.

"Obviously, she doesn't think we're serious."

Casey stopped and focused his alert brown eyes on Jamison. "Maybe she thinks she can outwit us," he said, running his hands through his hair. "If she does, she's wrong."

Casey's expression seemed to make Jamison uncomfortable. "You said she'd fold by now."

"Don't worry, she'll fold. You haven't seen Platt around have you?"

Jamison shook his head. "So what are we going to do?" he asked and put his hands in his pockets to hide his apparent nervousness.

Casey moved toward him and spoke in a low, controlled tone. "First, I'm going to find out where her children are, then I'm going to have Mr. Cross pay them another visit."

"You're not thinking of—"

"—No, Derek. I'm not going to kidnap them. I'm just going to turn up the heat a little."

"That may not be necessary," Jamison said, quickly. "They'll never make the board's numbers."

"Don't underestimate Taylor Zobrist," Casey returned.

"It's just that I don't want to go further than we have to," Jamison said, backing away from Casey.

"You focus on finding out what her people are up to. Let me take care of her family." Casey went back to the chair behind his desk, a signal he wanted to be alone. He wasn't happy with Jamison second-guessing him, which caused him to question the man's determination.

Casey picked up the phone and called Baci's for a reservation. For its preferred customers, Baci's would e-mail reservation confirmations to the addresses on file. Whenever Casey wanted to meet with Bamus, he would call Baci's and book a reservation in Alex's name. Alex would get the confirmation message and show up at the appointed time. Bamus did the same thing when he needed to meet with Casey.

He made the reservation for 9:00 P.M. at Baci's, which meant he and Bamus would meet in the bar at 8:30. All Casey needed was a few minutes with Bamus to convince him that it was time to question Dieter Wilkins directly.

Luckily, Casey thought to himself, Bamus's Brazilian security unit had managed to keep Wilkins and his girlfriend under surveillance, even after their attempt at a clandestine exit from São Paulo.

29

CHAPTER

The following morning, Taylor prepared a 10-point argument to convince Goodrich that a divergent organization was not only necessary in the short term for Carter-Crisp, but also vital to the company's long-term performance.

1. A company's ability to innovate consistently, maximize its learning from innovations, and continuously reposition itself through innovations depends on developing highly dynamic organizational capabilities from a broad range of sources: strategic alliances and partnerships with companies and universities, joint ventures, outsourcing to contractors, licensing of technologies from competitors, acquiring emerging technologies, franchising arrangements, and so forth. To accomplish this, companies need to create higher degrees of flexibility and autonomy in their organizations.
2. Experience in firms such as Hewlett-Packard, General Electric, Motorola, Unilever, and Procter &

Gamble suggests that part of R&D or new product development should be aligned with existing core businesses, while the other part(s) should operate independently from existing core businesses in order to maintain an unbiased, fresh, and long-term view.

3. The old idea of creating a sustainable competitive advantage is far too rigid for today's business environment and is being replaced by a new concept: creating and exploiting opportunities quickly and continuously. Accelerating creative breakthroughs requires a new vision for organizing and managing the innovation process.

4. When it comes to fostering continuous innovation, the most important ingredient is a culture of risk taking and mistake making that removes fear and allows people to develop a deeply rooted capability for constant innovation at all levels from the incremental to the ingenious.

5. Product extensions and continuous improvements (Perspective One innovations) are best achieved within the existing organization where all the necessary integration and coordination can be closely managed and guided through all facets of the company's existing operations.

6. Strategic value and cost exploitation (Perspective Two innovations)—where innovation depends on clearly understanding the organization's existing capabilities and leveraging them into new competitive advantages and market positions—can often be accelerated through consultants, think tanks, advertising agencies, and contract employees.

7. Capabilities expansion and acquisition (Perspective Three innovations) can be accelerated through outsourcing, acquisitions, joint ventures, licensing

arrangements, franchises, and other alliances because the basic idea of this level of innovation is to develop new talent and technology that can better meet customer needs and increase brand loyalty.

8. Revolutionary breakthroughs and fundamental change (Perspective Four innovations) can always be accelerated when the innovation process proceeds independently and autonomously from the rest of the organization. Although the idea of a virtual corporation that outsources everything has been generally oversold, it still works extremely well for this level of innovation.

9. The innovation path from idea to implementation can be greatly accelerated and facilitated when people are placed in an environment where their only responsibility is to drive their ideas forward to market introduction. More than anything else, this requires task-specific champions who can lead their teams through the various stages of product development: Perspective One innovations require organizational champions; Perspective Two innovations demand market/business champions; Perspective Three innovations need talent/technology champions; and Perspective Four innovations must have future champions.

10. The following graphic summarizes the divergent needs and orientations of Perspectives Two, Three, and Four innovation as compared with Perspective One innovation.

Taylor reviewed her list and notes one more time. She was ready. It took her a half hour to present all 10 points to Goodrich, who listened attentively. When she finished discussing her final point, she told Goodrich about her plan to

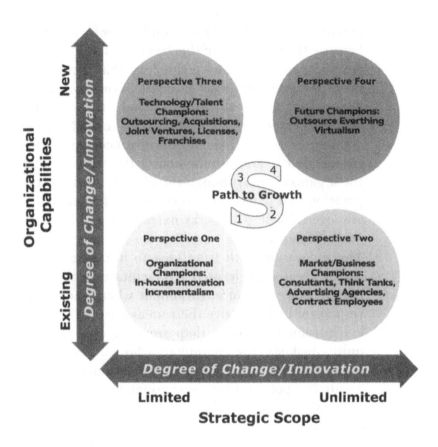

Organizational Capabilities

New

Existing

Degree of Change/Innovation

Perspective Three

Technology/Talent Champions: Outsourcing, Acquisitions, Joint Ventures, Licenses, Franchises

Perspective Four

Future Champions: Outsource Everthing Virtualism

Path to Growth

3 4

1 2

Perspective One

Organizational Champions: In-house Innovation Incrementalism

Perspective Two

Market/Business Champions: Consultants, Think Tanks, Advertising Agencies, Contract Employees

Degree of Change/Innovation

Limited   Unlimited

Strategic Scope

use Tom Platt and his firm to secure the location of the new divergent organization, which was yet to be identified. Then she told him it could cost the company from $7 million to $15 million.

Goodrich sat back in his red leather chair and looked pensive. His blue-green eyes softened when he spoke. "If that's what you need to make this happen, then I'll approve it."

Taylor stared in surprise at the seasoned CEO. She expected her proposal to be a tough sell and found his quick agreement unsettling. Even though she no longer suspected that he was involved with Nibblers or anyone else attempting to force the sale of Carter-Crisp Foods, she wondered if he'd given up hope. Was his acquiescence out of trust or desperation?

"I'm not trying to add to your stress by saying this," Goodrich said, as if he'd read her mind, "but you and your department *are* this company's last hope. The board has chosen to make innovation the deciding factor in whether they sell or hold on to their shares. And they're using the next ninety days, or I should say seventy-three days, as their empirical data. It's that simple. You and your team are the future of this company, and it's my job to make sure you have everything you need to succeed."

Goodrich continued as he stood up from behind his desk. "You know I'm retiring at the end of the year," he said, walking toward her.

Taylor nodded as she stood up and smoothed down the front of her gray slacks. Goodrich was now close enough that she could smell his Grey Flannel cologne mixed with the scent of age. It was the way her father used to smell.

Stopping a few inches from her face, Goodrich reached out and gently grasped her arms just below the shoulders. "I believe in you, Taylor. And I'm comfortable putting the company's future in your hands."

Was it possible he was suggesting she'd be his replacement? She knew she looked surprised. As she tried to find the right words, Goodrich continued.

"You understand what I'm saying, don't you?" he asked.

"Yes," she said weakly. Becoming the CEO of a consumer products company was something she'd dreamed about for a long time, but she never thought it might happen so soon. In his own way, Goodrich was communicating his lack of confidence in the other senior executives that made up Carter-Crisp's leadership team. Maybe more of them were involved in the scheme than she realized.

Back in her office, Taylor called Tom on his cell phone. "How are they?" she asked as soon as she heard his voice. She was anxious to learn anything about her children and mother.

"They're horseback riding and having a great time," Tom said. "I think your mother's enjoying it as much as the kids are."

She heard the whinny of a horse in the background. "Are you with them?"

"Of course. You think I'd miss an opportunity to contemplate the Grand Tetons from horseback?"

"Thank you, Tom," she said, her eyes watering.

"Do you want to talk to them?"

"No. I'll call them tonight. I just wanted to let you know that I'm moving most of my department out of the building to a new location, but we can talk about it later."

"What location do you have in mind?" Tom asked. Taylor heard him instruct his horse to halt.

"I was hoping you could help me with that. It obviously needs to be a place that can be secured. Everyone will maintain offices here as well. The question is how to do both without raising suspicions."

"Good question," Tom said. "Are you planning to group your people according to the four innovation perspectives?"

The question took Taylor completely by surprise. "Yes. How did you—?"

Tom cut her off. "I attended your retreat, remember. I may not have been there in person, but I was definitely listening. Seems to me there are some natural avenues for relocation, since you'll be depending on outside contractors," he said. "Each group could locate on the premises of its major contractor. That would lower suspicions about any absences from Carter-Crisp headquarters. The only thing we'd have to do is set up a work schedule that allows each group to maintain some regular presence at headquarters. I'm thinking out loud now. Maybe the Perspective Two group could locate in the building of a marketing company or strategic consulting firm. The Perspective Three group could locate on the premises of one of the manufacturing contractors or an engineering firm, and the Perspective Four group might locate at one of those business incubators or at an independent R&D facility. We'd just have to make sure that each location could be adequately secured and protected."

Taylor thought Tom's idea was brilliant. "That's perfect," she said, still surprised. "Can you make it work?"

"Absolutely. You select the contractors and make sure they have temporary space for your people. We'll secure their locations. If we run into any difficulties, we'll let you know before you move your people in."

"We have to move fast," Taylor said.

"How soon can you identify the contractors?"

"By the end of the day tomorrow."

"We'll have the locations secured within twenty-four hours after receiving your targets, unless we run into a problem," Tom told her. "I suggest you have backups for each location. Either way, your people will be able to move in before the weekend, but they'll need to be very careful about how they talk about this inside the company. How much are you going to tell them?"

"Just enough to let them know that we don't want the rest of the company knowing about our contracting arrangements or our innovation initiatives. The rationale is that the rest of the organization needs to stay focused on Perspective One innovation." Taylor paused. "Can you still see my kids?"

"Yeah, they're just entering Horseshoe Canyon. It's the best part of the trek."

"Tell them I love them and that I'll call them tonight."

30

CHAPTER

ieter looked up from the pages of the Elmore Leonard novel he was reading. The quail were running amid the swaying coconut trees on the Ilha de Comandatuba, an island resort located a few hundred yards off the coast of Salvador, Brazil. He watched the birds with pleasure from a hammock on the terrace of their beachside bungalow at the Hotel Transamerica. The resort was the largest in South America—nestled amid 250 acres of silken beaches, endless coconut trees, hibiscus, frangipani, and drenched in glorious, uninterrupted sunshine. It was one of the most beautiful places he'd ever seen.

This place was so beautiful that he and Angela had decided to stay for a week, maybe more. Despite this, Dieter was still worried about Taylor and Carter-Crisp, but the only thing he could do was respond to her requests. Late last night, he'd sent her an e-mail with every contact he could remember or identify that might help her create a divergent organization. Taylor's plan was an extremely ambitious and potentially dangerous one, but it might just work.

Behind him, the terrace doors to the bungalow opened. Angela wasn't expected back for a couple of hours, and he raised himself up and turned his head to look. Two men dressed in shorts and tank tops grabbed him by the arms and yanked him out of the hammock.

"Don't speak or your woman will die," the larger of the two men said.

The two men walked him arm in arm along a sandy path to the adjoining bungalow and pushed him through the opened terrace door.

"Sit down, Mr. Wilkins," said a third man dressed in slacks and a white shirt. He spoke without the accent of the other two, but he looked Brazilian. He pointed to a winged chair in the middle of the room.

One of the men behind him gave him a gentle push and he sat down. "What have you done with Angela," he barely managed to say.

"Nothing. She's still at the salon being pampered. And if you cooperate, we won't touch her. In fact, we'll leave you two lovebirds alone for the rest of your lives."

Dieter stared at the dark-haired, handsome man and then closed his eyes in an attempt to relieve the pounding in his head. "I'll do whatever you want, just don't touch Angela."

"Excellent. We'll have you back in your hammock before your Brazilian beauty returns. Now, Mr. Wilkins, tell us about Taylor Zobrist. How is she? And how are her lovely children?"

31

CHAPTER

By the end of the day on Tuesday, after numerous meetings and telephone calls, Taylor had identified her three locations. For Perspective Two, she opted for the regional headquarters in Long Beach of HomeService, a national home delivery company; for Perspective Three, the Irvine manufacturing facility of Dameco, a nitrogen packaging company from Germany; and, for Perspective Four, the San Diego headquarters of Barclays.com, an online book, music, and video retailer.

For better or worse, Taylor and her three assigned directors had been forced, somewhat prematurely, she thought, to establish each perspective's primary focus: home delivery for Perspective Two, nitrogen-sealed/self-heating packages for Perspective Three, and online snacks for Perspective Four. All the other initiatives identified at the retreat would still have to be aggressively pursued, but Taylor knew the location decisions would automatically favor some initiatives over others. If things worked out as she hoped, progress would be accelerated by reorganizing and relocating much of her department, yet she also knew there was always an increased risk when decisions were made so quickly. Maybe the added risk would spur her managers on to added effort, Taylor thought to herself.

She thought about calling Kate and Jeremy but decided to wait. Tom's people had reported to her that the phones at Carter-Crisp were still clean, but Tom had suggested not using them when conducting sensitive business. She prayed that the calls she and her directors had made to Home-Service, Dameco, and Barclays had not been tapped. Even if they had been intercepted, she said to herself, the full scope of their intentions could not have been discerned. The calls would simply point to the development of closer working relationships with three key contractors.

When she got home to her condo in Marina del Rey, she called the High Teton Ranch in Jackson Hole. After hearing about the day's glorious activities—Western fiction, pottery classes, moose watching, and river rafting—from Kate and Jeremy, Taylor talked with her mother who echoed the children's delight. Taylor was relieved, but more than a little disappointed that she couldn't be there with them. She asked her mother to put Tom on the phone.

"Wish you were here?" he asked in a playful voice.

"You know I do," she said, longing for her children more than ever.

"Give yourself a couple of weeks, and we'll get you back here for a few days."

"I'll need it by then," she said and sighed. She didn't want to admit that she missed Tom, too. "We've got our three locations with backups, if necessary." Taylor relayed her information—locations, operations, and key people at HomeService, Dameco, and Barclays—as Tom tapped and scratched onto his wireless Palm VII. When she was done, Tom assured her that he'd have the three sites surveyed and prepped by tomorrow.

"You're going to make it through this, Taylor. That's a promise," Tom said before saying good-bye and handing the phone over to Kate who was anxiously waiting to talk to her mother again.

The promise he had made was not a hollow one, Taylor hoped. He had assured her that her family was more than just another client. Getting things back to normal was now not only a professional priority, but also his number one personal concern. It made her smile.

32

CHAPTER

s soon as Casey entered Baci's Ristorante bar, Bamus stood up from his stool and went to the restroom. Casey followed.

"I think we're being watched," Bamus said when they were alone.

"Who is it?"

"The man in the tan sweater on the far side of the bar. He was here the last time we met. I may be getting paranoid, but I suggest we meet at Hennessey's in an hour. I'll leave first."

Casey nodded as another man entered the restroom.

An hour later, Casey and Bamus met at Hennessey's, a more secluded bar closer to the UCLA campus. There was no sign of the man in the tan sweater, but that didn't mean there weren't others, Casey thought to himself.

"Let's make this quick," Bamus said as he and Casey sat down at a just-emptied, high-top table in the corner of the crowded bar.

"What did you get from Dieter?" Casey asked, his eyes darting around the room.

"Taylor's setting up operations outside Carter-Crisp. She's planning to outsource everything, so she can hide the results from you and the rest of the company." Bamus sipped his beer.

"Did Dieter know where?" Casey leaned forward, resting his elbows on the table.

"No." Bamus reached inside his gray flannel blazer and produced two folded sheets of paper. He handed them to Casey. "Here's the list of the outsourcing contacts that Dieter sent to Taylor. With some research and a little investigation, your people should be able to find out what she's doing and where."

"What about her children?" Casey asked while still examining the list of outside contractors.

"He doesn't know where they are, and my people are sufficiently convinced he's telling the truth. However, he did say that Taylor's contingency escape plan would reunite her with her children within three hours."

"That means they're somewhere in the West," Casey said as he leaned back on his stool with a glint in his eye.

"Or in Mexico," Bamus returned. He'd already told Casey that he didn't like the idea of making more threats on Taylor's children because it was too risky.

"She wouldn't send them to Mexico. She's too paranoid about their well-being," Casey said before gulping down half his scotch and water.

"Find out where she's setting up her outsourcing command post, and then you can figure out how to slow her down."

Casey stared into the crowd. A waitress stopped by to see if the two men needed anything. She smiled, but he ignored her. He was still figuring out how long it might take to track down Taylor's children.

Bamus leaned closer to Casey and with an icy voice of warning said, "The last thing we need is an incident with one of Taylor's children to get out of control."

"Look, you've been calling the shots with Dieter from the beginning, and we still don't have a deal. Taylor is mine, and I'm going to make sure she doesn't meet the board's numbers."

This time Bamus was silent with a faraway look in his eyes.

Casey spoke suddenly, breaking the silence. "I suggest you use Dieter to get some more information from Taylor, including where her children are."

"I'll take care of Dieter. You make sure that Tom Platt can't make a connection between us and your people at Cross Associates," Bamus said as he stood up and put a twenty down on the table. "This is the last time we should meet in person. If you need to reach me, call me from the Los Angeles Athletic Club. I'll do the same."

Casey looked up at him, with an expression of resentment at Bamus's obvious attempt to distance himself from what the two of them had set in motion. "Don't worry about Cross. Taylor shredded the only evidence."

"Just make sure. You thought she fired Platt, too," Bamus said as he turned and walked away.

Casey drank the rest of his scotch and water as he monitored Bamus's exit from the crowded bar. He didn't expect to receive any additional help from the man. The sale of Carter-Crisp Foods was now up to him.

33

CHAPTER

$\mathcal{D}$uring the next two weeks, Taylor put in 16-hour days to give each of her four innovation groups the attention they wanted and needed. Progress was slow, and Taylor began to seriously question whether they'd even have a chance of making it past the $25 million and $5 million not-to-exceed marks that David Cross had identified in his threatening note.

Maybe it was just as well, all things considered, then she reminded herself that her children were safe. The people who threatened her thought they could get away with scaring her into submission, but they couldn't, and wouldn't, she told herself, again.

The Perspective One group was moving along steadily and predictably toward introducing an extra-cheese nacho chip, a heavy-duty barbeque potato chip, a miniature pretzel pack to price under $0.50, a resealable chip package, a larger snack assortment pack for schools and club stores, and a two-for-one promotion package on all canned salsas, spreads, and dips, just as planned. Taylor felt confident about the group's ability to reach its targets of $22 million in sales and $4.6 million in profits.

But building effective working relationships with the outside contractors in the other three groups was turning out to be more difficult and demanding than anticipated. She could already see the effects of the strain on her people. Tempers flared more than usual and the sarcasm was growing. If one of the three more radical innovation groups didn't come up with a major breakthrough soon, she wasn't sure her people would be able to maintain their work schedules or their concentration.

Even the most gifted creative people, Taylor knew, could only sustain their concentration for so long, before needing to have their batteries recharged by some sort of breakthrough. Just as it began to look like it would never happen, it did. Like a burst of revelation from Heaven, there was a breakthrough at Dameco by the Perspective Three group, and it was better than anyone expected.

It was late Sunday morning when Taylor received the news. She had just finished talking on the telephone with her kids in Jackson Hole and a sense of hopelessness had begun to engulf her. Then the phone rang.

She picked it up quickly, thinking it might be her children calling back.

"We got it to work!" came the excited voice over the phone.

"Brad?" Taylor said, recognizing the voice of Brad Strauss, director of the Perspective Three innovation group.

"Yeah. We've been working nonstop since yesterday morning on the self-heating problem. We got it to work, and it doesn't compromise the food seal. The heat gets activated when you open the snack package. Even if you rip open the package the wrong way, the worst thing that happens is you have to open the heating pouch separately. It's easy and there's no way to contaminate the food."

"Are you sure?" Taylor said, holding her breath. Brad and his team had chosen Dameco because of its nitrogen packaging capability. Nitrogen was injected into a flexible aluminum package during the sealing process to remove all the oxygen so that meat, sauces, cheeses, bakery rolls, and other perishable foods could be moist-packed for a shelf life of up to nine months without spoiling, drying out, or becoming stale. Dameco was the only company in the world that had perfected the nitrogen packaging process and, for the past two years, it had been selling one of its products—a pepperoni stick baked in a soft roll—at unusually high volumes for such items in Germany.

Luckily for Carter-Crisp, Dameco was a small family-owned company that didn't want to get gobbled up by a huge global corporation, so it had come to the United States a year ago in search of a like-minded strategic partner. The company's founders met Dieter Wilkins at a snack food trade show and quickly struck up a relationship that eventually led to a joint venture.

Unfortunately, the first Carter-Crisp/Dameco product introduction—a calzone snack with pepperoni, tomato sauce, and cheese baked in a soft roll—had been a big flop because the extended shelf life of the nitrogen-sealed packaging wasn't enough of a selling point to capture consumer interest. In the days after the Santa Barbara retreat, Brad and his team had decided to work with Dameco to combine nitrogen packaging and self-heating. It was a risk that involved two new capabilities for Carter-Crisp and one for Dameco, but Brad and his team had become so singularly focused on developing the new capabilities that they had become fearless, and that's when the breakthrough occurred.

Their approach was simple, yet difficult to execute. They applied current disposable hand-warmer technology—iron,

151

water, cellulose, vermiculite, carbon, and salt activated by exposure to oxygen through a permeable polypropylene bag that heats to 160 degrees Fahrenheit—by double-wrapping a heating bag around a moist snack that could include meats, cheeses, sauces, vegetables, and soft bakery rolls. The breakthrough was born when the team devised a way to activate the heating pouch at the moment the package was opened. The customer simply had to reclose the package using the resealable feature, wait for two minutes while the snack heated, and then eat the fresh, moist, warm snack.

"We've already tested it dozens of times to make sure. This is real, Taylor. This one's going to make Carter-Crisp a helluva lot of money," Brad exclaimed.

"Has Clancey looked at it?" Taylor asked, still afraid to believe this was as good as it sounded. It wasn't that she didn't trust Brad, but so much was riding on a major breakthrough that could turbocharge everything. Dr. Bernard M. Clancey was Carter-Crisp's chief scientist and a trained microbiologist. His job was to make sure that every product the company produced was absolutely safe.

"He's been right here every step of the way. We agreed not to call you until he gave us the green light," Brad returned excitedly.

"This is exactly what we needed to keep us going. Congratulations, Brad. Is everybody still there?"

"They're all here, waiting to hear your response. We want to begin gearing up for production this afternoon, as soon as we have your okay."

"Tell them I'll be there within the hour. I want to do this in person." Taylor was elated, but she also knew this marked the beginning of an execution nightmare, and a heightened security risk. As soon as she put down the phone, she called Tom Platt to tell him.

Taylor showered, dressed, and got in her Volvo station wagon. She drove to the American Novelties store on Sepulveda Boulevard to pick up a few party accessories and humorous toys for Brad's team. The small gesture would communicate, she hoped, her enormous gratitude.

Inside the store, a man bumped into her and knocked what she had taken from the shelf out of her hands. He was apologetic and helped her pick up the finger skateboards and glow necklaces that had fallen to the floor. Taylor thanked him and thought nothing more about it; she was anxious to see Brad and his team. Minutes later, she was on the 405 freeway traveling south toward Irvine.

34

CHAPTER

om Platt was already waiting in the Dameco parking lot, watching from inside a blue delivery van, when Taylor arrived. He had doubled the number of people monitoring the three new locations from 12 to 24, 8 at each facility, because of several recent attempts to infiltrate electronically and physically. Unfortunately, none of the perpetrators had been detected in time to apprehend them. And, even though each facility had been wired to inhibit any electronic surveillance, no system was ever foolproof.

As Tom watched Taylor get out of her car and walk to the building's entrance, his three-man crew in the delivery truck began picking up a high-frequency surveillance probe coming from Taylor's direction. Platt immediately punched a button on the console in front of him and began talking to one of his people outside the van.

"Anything unusual happen at the store?" Tom asked.

"She was inside for less than ten minutes."

"Did you follow her inside?"

There was a pause on the line. "I went in as soon as other customers began arriving, just as we agreed."

"How many after her?" Tom asked, growing more concerned.

"Twelve. Nine women and children and three men."

"Did you pick up any surveillance readings while she was in the store or after she left?"

"Nothing."

"Where are you now?"

"Across the street from the Dameco building."

"Keep me posted if you see anything," Tom said. "I'm going inside. Taylor's got a bug on her."

Tom grabbed a large black bag from one of the stainless-steel cabinets, quickly exited the van, and hurried to the building's entrance. Once inside, he whisked the magnetic strip of his new Dameco identification card across the magnetic reader. The sliding-glass-and-metal doors opened and he rushed toward the laboratory area.

After he passed through another set of security doors, he entered the experimental lab and kitchen area. Taylor was giving high fives and hugs to her people. He walked toward her. "Taylor, sorry to interrupt the celebration," he said, his voice low, "but can I talk to you for a moment?"

"What's wrong?" Taylor asked. He saw a look of terror on her face. "Has something happened to the children?"

"No," Tom said, raising his index finger to his lips and making it clear that she shouldn't say another word. He took her by the arm and started walking toward the main corridor. "I only need her for a few minutes," he said over his shoulder to the group of 20 or so people milling around one of the long lab tables.

When they reached the main corridor, Tom took Taylor to the women's rest room, took a blank index card from his jacket, and wrote the following note: "*Take your clothes off, including shoes and jewelry. Put them in the bag and bring it to me. I'll wait right here.*"

Taylor read the note and then looked at Tom in astonishment.

He handed her the black, copper-lined bag and nodded toward the rest room door.

Taylor quickly removed her clothes, shoes, and jewelry. Because the rest room was so close to the laboratory, there was a changing room with lockers and disposable lab smocks. She stuffed her linen jacket, blouse, slacks, and undergarments into the bag on top of her shoes and jewelry. Then she put on a blue disposable smock and took the bag of clothes to Tom, who was standing outside the door.

Tom smiled coyly as he took the bag. This was certainly no time to be playful, he knew, but later he'd comment on the smock. "I'll be back in five minutes." He rushed out of the building to the delivery truck where he and his three associates combed every inch of her clothing with their handheld detecting instruments. They found two very small bugs, one-fifth the size of a dime, attached with sticky adhesive to the inside of her jacket's side pocket and on the inside of her shoe's heel.

Tom looked at the two men and the woman standing next to him as he dropped the two bugs into an alcohol solution inside a thick stainless-steel, copper-lined container and screwed on the cap. "These bugs are state-of-the-art and very expensive," he said. He placed the container on the shelf. "Find out who manufactures and distributes them. Maybe we can uncover a path to our surveillants."

"We're still getting a reading from inside the building," the woman said.

Tom grabbed the bag of clothes, returned to the rest room, and gave it to Taylor.

"What's going on?" she asked as soon as she emerged from the rest room dressed.

Tom ran his handheld detector along her body from head to toe. There was nothing indicating another bug. "There were two tiny electronic bugs on your clothing, one inside your jacket pocket and the other on the heel of your shoe," he said.

"How?"

"That's what I need to ask you. Did you have contact with anyone in the novelty store?"

"No. Just the sales clerk," Taylor said. They began walking back toward the lab, and then she stopped. "Wait! There was a man who bumped into me when I was getting some things off a shelf. He was very unassuming and nice. He helped me pick up everything."

"Pick what up?"

"The finger skateboards and glow necklaces that fell on the floor."

"Where are they?"

"In the lab, in a bag. I didn't have a chance to distribute them."

"Go back to your people. Let me take the bag. I'll bring it to you as soon as we've had a chance to examine it."

Taylor nodded as they entered the lab area. After pointing out the bag of novelties to Tom, she turned her attention to Brad's team of innovators. The fear inside her was rising, but she tried not to let it show.

Back in the delivery van, Tom and his crew found two more bugs attached to the axles of two of the finger skateboards. After disposing of them and making sure there were no more indications of electronic surveillance, Tom returned the novelties to Taylor and the Perspective Three team in the laboratory. He watched, admiringly, as she lavished her people with praise and distributed her sack of toys, each with a symbolic message. The glow necklaces were for keeping the fire burning; the kaleidoscope key chains were for envisioning nothing but success; the finger skateboards were for negotiating the twists and turns of implementation; the porcupine balls were for remaining vigilant and invincible; and the baby kick balls were for scoring the ultimate goal. But Tom knew she was scared to death.

She needs a break, he thought. But first, he had to find out if she'd made any telephone calls while she was driving from the novelty store to Dameco. Thanks to the inhibiting equipment his people had installed inside the Dameco facility, he wasn't overly concerned about whether the eavesdroppers had heard anything after she entered the building, but he was concerned about what she might have said in a telephone conversation or to herself while driving in the car.

Thirty minutes later, after Taylor had been through several successful demonstrations of the new self-heating package, she walked over to where Tom was standing. As they walked down to the building's main foyer, she thanked him for being there.

"Tell me I'm doing the right thing," she said.

"After watching you in there today, I can see why Goodrich has such confidence in you."

"That wasn't my question."

"If you're asking me whether we can keep you and your family safe, yes, I think we can. But not without risk, and it's obviously growing. My people are trying to track down where the bugs came from. American Novelties has three cameras that may have video-taped the man who bumped into you. We're doing everything. But if you're asking me whether the risk is worth it, I can't answer that. Only you can."

"I'm asking you what you think," Taylor said as she looked directly into his eyes.

The gaze made him feel both uneasy and flattered. He was becoming more and more attracted to her, but he couldn't let his personal feelings affect his professional judgment. "I think you're doing the right thing. And you're doing it very well."

She touched his arm and squeezed gently. "Thank you."

He wanted to take her in his arms and hug her, but he suppressed the thought. The last thing he needed was to get emotionally involved with a client. Besides, he'd already learned from watching the personal heartache of colleagues and going through his own miserable breakup with a fiancée that his line of work had little sympathy for romantic relationships or familial bonds. "I need to ask you something," he said.

"Go ahead."

"Did you talk to anyone on the phone while you were driving from the novelty store to Dameco or did you talk to yourself out loud?"

Suddenly, Taylor's entire countenance changed. He could see the fear she'd managed to suppress come flooding back with a vengeance. "I called the ranch," she whispered as her face turned ashen.

"Who did you talk to?"

Taylor began acting faint and leaned on Tom to steady herself. "I talked to Freddie, the owner of the ranch. Mother and the kids were still at church. I told her to tell the kids I'd call them later this afternoon." Freddie was one of the owners of the High Teton Ranch and its chief hostess.

"Did either of you mention the name of the ranch?"

Taylor told him what Freddie had said—"*Jackson's favorite dude ranch, how can I help you?*" She had led them straight to her children.

"Let's go," Tom said, putting his arm around Taylor and guiding her to the front door.

"What are we going to do?"

"We're going to Jackson Hole," Tom said in a matter-of-fact voice that belied his own fear.

35

CHAPTER

"hey're at a dude ranch near Jackson Hole, Wyoming. We don't have an exact location yet, but we're working on it," Cross said from inside his surveillance-equipped SL600 Mercedes-Benz roadster.

"Are the bugs still in place?" Casey asked over the phone from his Santa Monica beach house. David Cross came at a high price, but he was worth every dollar.

"No. Platt detected them as soon as she arrived at Dameco."

"Did we get any lead on what they're working on?"

"Only that it's some sort of a packaging breakthrough."

"Now what?" Casey asked, knowing that they didn't have much time before Platt reacted to the breach Cross had achieved.

"I'm on my way to Jackson Hole to renew my acquaintance with Jeremy," Cross said in a cold, detached voice.

"I only want you to scare her out of the picture. Nothing else," Casey said. He recalled his last encounter with Bamus and felt for the first time that things could easily get out of control.

"Don't worry. We know exactly how far to push these sorts of things without causing irreparable damage. We need to send a message to Taylor that we're still around and can infiltrate her protection any time we choose. My people are already in the air and should be in Jackson within the hour. I'm leaving in a few minutes. I want to be the one who talks to Jeremy."

"What do you think Platt will do?"

"Close ranks around the children, then move them as soon as possible."

"What if this doesn't scare her off?"

"We'll make sure she knows this is her last warning." He paused. "We're prepared to go as far as you want."

Cross's words sank in deep. For an instant, he wondered whether things had already gone too far, making it impossible to ever marry Carter-Crisp and Nibblers. He assured himself it was still possible, in spite of Tom Platt and his people. They'd never be able to prove anything.

He walked to the balcony windows overlooking the ocean. He wasn't happy. His cash reserves were dwindling because of Cross's exorbitant fees, the risks were escalating, and he was growing more and more impatient. This cat-and-mouse game needed to end, and end soon, before the board changed its mind about Carter-Crisp's ability to innovate . . . and before it was too late to consummate a deal.

36

CHAPTER

A s soon as Jeremy Zobrist changed his clothes after church, he ran to see Duncan, a 15-year-old palomino and his favorite horse at the High Teton Ranch. The horse stables had a wide aisle down the center with 10 stalls on each side. Duncan was in number three, about 20 feet from the front.

Two of Platt's people followed Jeremy, remaining about 15 feet outside, yet with a clear view of the boy. They had been fully alerted about the breach and were taking the necessary precautions. No member of Taylor's family would be out of their sight for even a moment, but they were trained to do their jobs discretely and not draw undue attention to themselves.

Jeremy perched on the top rung of a stall ladder and fed the yellow and white palomino from a sack of oats. Duncan was the gentlest horse on the ranch, but even so, Jeremy had clearly demonstrated to the ranch hands that he knew how to act around horses. He stroked Duncan's forehead between the ears and eyes as the horse nibbled and licked the oats from his other hand.

Earlier, his grandmother had told him to pack his bags because they were leaving the ranch when his mother came. When he asked where they were going, and whether they'd be coming back, she told him she didn't know. He promised his grandmother he would pack his bag as soon as he said good-bye to Duncan. Jeremy was glad he was going to see his mother, but he wasn't happy about leaving his favorite horse. This had been his best summer ever. He looked out the stable entrance and saw the man and woman under a spreading oak tree where they could get out of the sun. They were Tom's friends—the ones who were always watching him. He felt safe.

"I've got some apples, if you want them." The voice came from the stall opposite Duncan's.

When Jeremy turned, he froze. It was the man from the marina—the one who had invited him to go sailing—dressed as a ranch hand. "No. I don't want any apples," he said softly, his heart beating fast.

"No apples then. I'm here to give you a message for your mother." The man paused. "You can tell her when she arrives."

Jeremy began to climb down from his perch. He remembered what his mother had told him to do if he saw the man again. *Run for help.* He remembered Tom's friends under the tree.

"You and I both know that you could scream right now and your two friends outside would be in here within seconds," the man said. "It's your mother who's in danger, Jeremy. There are people at my company who want your mother to fail at her job. It's very sad and very wrong, but true. I don't know whom to trust anymore."

Jeremy stopped. His mother in danger. He was torn between running and listening to what the man had to say. What he couldn't figure out was where the other ranch hands had gone when there were usually three or four of them in the stables. In fact, he'd never seen it empty before.

"I don't know whose side anyone's on," the man said, nodding to the couple outside. "That's why I need to warn your mother." Cross tossed one apple to Jeremy and then a second. "Feed those to your horse and I'll give you my message for your mother."

Jeremy saw the woman start to walk toward him until she saw him catch the two apples from a ranch hand and return to Duncan's stall. She turned and went back to stand under the tree again. He shoved one of the apples through the wood slats and into Duncan's chomping mouth.

"Listen carefully, but don't look back at me," Cross said from inside the other stall. "Your mother's friend Tom Platt and his people—and that includes the two outside—work for my company. Your mother doesn't know it, but you and Kate could be kidnapped by them at any moment. That's the message, Jeremy. Tell your mother as soon as you see her, but don't tell anyone else, not even your sister. I'll be here as long as I can, if you need me. But this will probably be the last time I'll have a chance to warn you."

The words left Jeremy scared, and unsure of what to do. What if the man was telling the truth? He fed the second apple to Duncan and then turned to leave the stables. His grandmother would be waiting for him.

"Just remember. I'm here if you need me."

Jeremy remembered how he'd felt on the boat. He began to run, hard, toward the ranch house.

37
CHAPTER

s the Gulfstream V landed at the Jackson Airport, Jeremy's stomach churned with anxiety. Nothing really made sense—leaving school two weeks early, leaving the ranch, and now the man from the marina that day—but he knew his mother would take care of things when he told her what had happened. He couldn't imagine Tom Platt being a bad guy. He liked Tom, and his mother trusted him, but the man in the stables had scared him; what if he was right about Tom?

Jeremy ran as soon as the door to the private jet opened. His mother met him at the base of the stairs. They hugged each other, and then, barely able to catch his breath, Jeremy unloaded everything he'd been holding inside.

Taylor was outraged. She dropped to her knees and held her son tight. This was the very thing she had feared the most, and yet, she'd allowed it to happen again. Even Tom's people had failed her. She thought about the people responsible for this brutality—and that's exactly what it was, she told herself as she looked into her son's eyes—brutality. They wouldn't let her quit or go to the police, and she wasn't going to let them get away with it.

Tears streamed down her son's cheeks, mingling with her own as she pressed his face to hers. That's when she made the decision not to leave her children again until this was over—which meant not going back to Carter-Crisp Foods—at least, physically.

Thirty minutes later, after the jet had been refueled and the two pilots filed the necessary flight plan, Taylor and her family and Tom Platt were on their way to a new hideaway. Once the aircraft had reached its cruising altitude of 40,000 feet, flying southwest toward Los Angeles, Tom called a personal friend, Alan Montgomery, chief of the FBI's Chicago Bureau. The two of them had started their careers together at the NSA. A few years later they both left, Tom for the private sector and Alan for the FBI, but they'd always remained close. Within minutes the Gulfstream V was on a new northeasterly course to Chicago.

Tom arranged for the flight record to show the Gulfstream V returning to LAX while actually flying to O'Hare's executive terminal. In exchange for the favor, Tom promised to bring Montgomery and the FBI up to speed on everything as soon as they landed.

As they flew to Chicago, Taylor told her family about everything that had happened over the past several weeks. Kate, Jeremy, and her mother Eileen had lots of questions, which Taylor and Tom answered in detail.

Jeremy looked at Tom uncertainly. "The man at the stables said you were one of the bad guys," he blurted out, angrily. "How do we know you're not?"

Tom glanced at Taylor and then leaned toward the boy. "Because it's not true." His voice was calm but firm. "And you're just going to have to trust me on that one. I care about your family, Jeremy. I'm here to help you."

"Why did he tell me his company was doing something wrong?" Jeremy asked.

"Because he wanted you to believe he was good," Tom said. "He was right about Nibblers trying to buy Carter-Crisp Foods and your mother being in danger. But he lied about me, and he lied about himself. He's no friend."

"Why did he pick me?"

"He knew that contacting you would scare your mother more than if he contacted her directly. Does that make sense?"

Jeremy nodded, and the discussion quickly turned to what they would be doing for the rest of the summer. Kate wanted to know if she could invite one of her friends, and Jeremy wanted to know if there would be horses at the new place.

A few minutes later, Tom left for the front of the aircraft to begin making the necessary arrangements for accommodations. He knew the Chicago area well, and, based on what he'd heard from Taylor's children, he'd already targeted a couple of resort cottages on Lake Juno in southwestern Michigan where there was sailing, fishing, and horseback riding.

Taylor reassured her children that she would not be leaving them again, as she helped them find a video to watch on their personal TV consoles. But she wondered how she was going to manage her four innovation groups from long distance. Until the people who were responsible for the threats and the surveillance were in jail, she would have no choice but to work from Chicago, Lake Juno, or wherever they ended up. She couldn't let them get to her children again or thwart the successful implementation of her team's recent breakthrough. She reassured herself that she was doing the right thing.

It took her 20 minutes sitting by herself at the back of the plane to make the mental transition back to self-heating snack packages. But she had to, and when she did, it was with an intensified concentration that seemed fueled, she thought, by nothing more than sheer adrenaline and a mother's will to protect her children.

Her mind turned to Harvard economist Joseph Schumpeter's words *creative destruction*. She'd used the words at the retreat when describing Perspective Four innovation. The two McKinsey consultants who authored the book by the same name described creative destruction as clearing the ground for new creation. It was true, revolutionary change always involved some sort of personal, cultural, or operational destruction: Out with the old and in with the new, but how old was old when you were in the middle of a breakthrough?

As she pondered the question, wondering what she needed to destroy or remove or deconstruct in order to clear the path for implementing Brad's self-heating breakthrough, it began to dawn on her that the four perspectives she'd created and used to organize her people might be the single biggest obstacle to implementation, precisely because they were divergent, not convergent, efforts.

In one of those rare "eureka" moments, flying 40,000 feet above the plains of Iowa, her mind's eye envisioned the entirety of the problem, the solution, and the outcome in one glorious revelation. Separating her people into the four perspective groups—each one representing a distinctly different type and level of innovation—had facilitated and accelerated Brad's transformational breakthrough, the incremental advances in the Perspective One group, and the progress, albeit slow, in the other two groups.

However, continued separation, in terms of thinking, organizing, and operating, after achieving a major breakthrough in one of the perspective groups could prevent full realization of the breakthrough's potential, thus compromising its successful implementation. She'd been right to isolate the four perspectives as a way of accelerating breakthroughs. Now she had to combine the perspectives to implement Brad's breakthrough. Every perspective deserves a breakthrough and a breakthrough deserves every perspective, she told herself.

Taylor looked out the window at the twilight sky, imagining the letter S superimposed over a large apple tree complete with roots. The S path to growth had suddenly taken on a whole new meaning: The S not only meant simultaneous pursuit of innovation in all four perspectives, it also meant simultaneous support from all four perspectives, and that's what Brad Strauss and his team needed now to realize the full potential of their breakthrough, particularly support from Perspectives Two and Four. Specifically, they needed a quick way to test-market a wide range of self-heating snacks (i.e., Perspective Four's online snack testing centers) and a quick way to distribute them to consumers (i.e., Perspective Two's home delivery).

She'd leave Perspective One out of the mix for now because of the ongoing surveillance, but with a little preparation, the Perspective Two and Perspective Four groups could easily adapt their innovation agendas to support self-heating snacks. That way, when the first batch came off the Dameco assembly line, they'd be tested and marketed through Barclays.com and distributed through HomeService. It was a beautiful idea, and a breakthrough in its own right. If she could just pull it off.

When Tom sat down next to Taylor in the back of the plane to give her an update on the housing arrangements, she reached over and grabbed his arm, clenching it tightly. "I just had one of those Mozart moments," she said, feeling slightly embarrassed but wanting to share her experience.

"Mozart moments?" Tom had a boyish grin on his face.

"You know. One of those moments when everything comes together and you see it all right in front of you, or hear it all, in Mozart's case."

"Tell me more," Tom said, inching closer.

"I can't begin to tell you how grateful I am for what you've—"

"First, tell me more about Mozart and your moment of everything coming together."

Taylor smiled at him. "You know how Mozart composed music, don't you?"

"No idea," he said smiling.

"Yes, you do." She realized he was playing with her.

"Well, maybe a little idea, but I'd like to hear your version."

Taylor reached into her purse and pulled out her handheld Compaq iPAQ, which she rarely used except for storing favorite quotes and new ideas. She tapped in the retrieval sequence and then handed the pocket PC to Tom. "This should refresh your memory," she said.

Tom read the quote from the screen.

When I feel well and in good humour, or when I am taking a drive or walking after a good meal, or in a night when I cannot sleep, thoughts crowd into my mind as easily as you could wish. Where do they come from? I do not know and I have nothing to do with it.

Those which please me I keep in my head and hum them; at least others have told me that I do so. Once I have my theme, another melody comes linking itself with the first one in accordance with the needs of the composition as a whole; the counterpoint, the parts for each instrument and all the melodic fragments at last produce the complete work.

Then my soul is on fire with inspiration. The work grows; I keep expanding it, conceiving more and more clearly until I have the entire composition finished in my head although it may be long. Then my mind seizes it, as a glance of my eye would a beautiful picture or a handsome youth. It does not come to me successively, with various parts worked out in detail, as they will later on, but it is in its entirety that my imagination lets me hear it.

Wolfgang Amadeus Mozart

"So what was your moment like?" Tom asked.

"I saw the entire innovation process in a single picture."

"What did it look like?"

"A tree," Taylor said, smiling.

"A tree? Are you being serious?"

"Yes," she said. "It was an apple tree with roots, trunk, branches, leaves, and fruit. The roots were the imagining process, the trunk was the integrating process, the branches were the isolating process, and the leaves and fruit were the illuminating result. The four stages of innovation—imagine, integrate, isolate, and illuminate—combined with the four perspectives of innovation—incremental, insightful, inventive, and ingenious—along the S path to growth. They're the eight *I*'s of innovation, performed simultaneously and supportively." She laughed.

Tom laughed, too, and looked at her with admiration. In the midst of uncertainty and danger, she was still playful and brilliant. He was getting more and more hooked by this woman. "Keep going," he said, shifting positions and brushing against her shoulder. The feeling of touching her again was definitely exhilarating.

"Imagining occurs deep underground as the trunk of the tree divides into root systems representing different perspectives in search of breakthroughs. Some roots draw from shallow ground and others dig much deeper. We used four fundamentally different perspectives for our root system at the retreat, but you could use as many as you needed. Integrating takes place above the ground between imagining and isolating to ensure that the branches get the full benefit of all the roots and vice versa. Once a breakthrough has been identified in one of the perspectives, it has to be united with the other perspectives to realize its full potential and value. Getting tired yet?"

"Not a chance," he said, earnestly.

"Isolating happens along a multitude of branches where you continue drawing upon all four perspectives to isolate obstacles, barriers, and hindrances to implementation and replace them with supportive processes. Some of the old branches have to be destroyed while new branches are grafted in. Illuminating occurs as the leaves sprout, the fruit ripens, and consumers are stimulated to buy. Everything that proved successful along the path to innovation must be illuminated to promote further innovation. That's it. That was my Mozart moment."

Tom leaned over the console between them and slid his fingers into a clasp of Taylor's hand. "You're a remarkable woman, and I'm not going anywhere until I make sure you get through this with flying colors."

There were still plenty of obstacles to overcome in the days and weeks ahead, Taylor thought as she looked into Tom's eyes, but she felt surprisingly calm and confident. "Thank you, Tom," she said as she squeezed his hand.

38

CHAPTER

hen Taylor didn't show up at work for the entire week, Casey was ecstatic. The second encounter at the dude ranch in Jackson Hole had definitely worked, he told himself.

With Taylor Zobrist out of the picture, it was only a matter of time before Carter-Crisp Foods succumbed to Nibblers. The thought made his head buzz with anticipation. He called his administrative assistant to tell her she could leave early. It was Friday afternoon and time to celebrate.

The Crobar, between Malibu and Topanga Beach, was the first dance club that came to mind. He hadn't been there in weeks, and the thought of finding a fresh new face enthralled him. Obsessing over his problems in recent weeks had seriously dampened his sexual appetite, but not anymore.

Things were turning around, he told himself as he walked to the parking garage and climbed into his Porsche. He slid the gearshift into first and pulled out onto Beverly Boulevard, leaving two long black streaks of burned rubber on the road.

Several hours later, as Casey guided Heather, his new love interest, from the balcony to the bedroom at his Santa Monica beach house, there was a knock at the front door. He looked at his watch. Who was knocking at his door at one in the morning? Casey told Heather to make herself comfortable. He'd be right back.

Casey looked through the peephole at Derek Jamison. "What happened?" he asked as he opened the door and let the man in.

"I finally got one of Taylor's people to talk about what they're doing at Dameco. I've been trying to reach you for the past two hours," Jamison said.

"I turned off my phones." Casey felt the panic rise inside him. "Give me a minute."

Casey went to the bedroom and told Heather he needed to talk to one of his colleagues about an emergency at work. She told him to hurry, but he could already feel the passion seeping out of him. When he got back to Jamison, he led him out the balcony door and down the stairs to the beach. "Tell me everything," he said.

"They've created a self-heating package," Jamison told him as they trudged through the soft sand to the water. "According to Carl Ramage, their group decided that nitrogen packaging wasn't enough, so they combined it with self-heating. You've always talked about it as the next big breakthrough, but I never thought these guys would pull it off, and certainly not now."

Casey's heart sank and his gut tightened. This was the last thing he expected Taylor's group to tackle. Introducing a self-heating snack pack was precisely what he'd planned to do as CEO of Carter-Crisp, but of course, he hadn't yet had the chance. "The joint venture that Dieter set up with Dameco is one of the main reasons Nibblers wants to get its hands on

Carter-Crisp. They want Dameco's technological know-how," Casey said in a somber voice.

The two men walked in silence.

"Does it work?" Casey asked, as they reached the ocean's edge.

"Carl wouldn't divulge any of the details, but judging by the look on his face, it does—and better than anyone expected."

Casey wanted to scream in frustration. But he needed to remain calm and take action quickly, before this deal and his life slipped out of his hands. He thought of the two marketing principles that had been guiding him over the past few months. One principle was defensive: Aggressive moves should always be blocked. The other principle was offensive: Attack at the point of weakness. That's what he'd been doing and that's what he had to continue doing. "How did you get Carl to talk?"

"A group of us met at Swani's for beers. After five or six, he started talking until he realized he'd said too much."

"Can you find out when they're going to market?"

"Not from Carl. He left the bar when I started asking questions. But now I know who else is in his group."

"What about the other groups?"

"Nothing."

Casey took a long, final gaze at the surf as it crashed along the shore. The nausea that had engulfed him was slowly turning into resolve. He turned and began walking back toward the beach house. "Get some sleep, Derek. It's going to be a long weekend. Meet me in the office at seven."

Casey returned to Heather who was waiting patiently. With a controlled coolness that surprised even himself, he apologized to Heather, telling her that an emergency at work demanded his immediate attention.

He drove her to her apartment, kissed her good night, and asked for a rain check. Then he drove north on the Pacific Coast Highway to clear his head. There was no way his calculating mind would let his body sleep tonight, not when new plans had to be devised, and devised quickly.

39

CHAPTER

*A*ll 16 of Taylor's directors and managers from Perspectives Two, Three, and Four, along with Goodrich and a half-dozen managers and executives from Dameco, were present Saturday morning at the Irvine facility when Nathan Goodrich ripped open the new self-heating package. The group watched anxiously as he resealed the package and waited two minutes before taking a bite of the hot beef-and-bean burrito with cheese and salsa.

"Terrific," he said as a burst of applause and whistles erupted from the group. He took another bite. "This is delicious."

Goodrich ripped open another package, this time containing a mini–barbeque chicken sandwich. After the two-minute heating time, he took a bite. "Taylor, I think you and your people, and of course, with the help of Dameco's packaging prowess, have just created a revolutionary new future for Carter-Crisp Foods."

There was another round of applause and shouts before Taylor spoke into the videoconferencing camera from the veranda of the summer cottage on Lake Juno, near Edwardsburg, Michigan. "There's more, Nathan." The room grew silent as everyone looked at the 60-inch television monitor projecting Taylor's smiling face.

Taylor continued. "Not only do we have ten more snacks for you to sample, we also want to show you how these snacks will be introduced to the market. We're not doing anything in the same old way. Nothing about this product line will be conventional. We're going to market over the Internet, distribute through home delivery, and build a new brand called *snackcity.com*." Taylor paused for a moment. There was an eruption of applause and whistling. "Snackcity.com will be a web site where you can taste-test experimental snacks through a home delivery service within 60 minutes of logging on in most urban areas, make suggestions for new snack concepts, place orders, provide specific feedback on snacks, obtain detailed nutritional information, read reviews on snacks, send snacks to friends, enter snack contests, play snack games, have snack chats, and become as immersed as you'd like in the new world of snacks. I'm meeting with Zacharman Partners in Chicago this afternoon to begin working on the advertising campaign."

There was another eruption of applause and whistling when Taylor finished. "We're behind you all the way," Goodrich said to more applause and shouting.

For the next hour, Taylor's three directors took Goodrich through the details of how the snackcity.com strategy would work while he taste-tested a variety of experimental snacks— pizzas, calzones, tacos, hamburgers, nachos, eggs and bacon, pasta, seafood dumplings, and yakisobi—all contained in self-heating packages. Taylor's people and the Dameco team had been working around the clock to get ready for Goodrich's visit.

As Taylor stared at the computer screen, watching her directors make their presentations to Goodrich, she longed to be there in person. But every time she glanced at her two children on the lake in a fishing boat with Tom Platt, she knew this was where she needed to be, at least for now.

She wished she could tell everyone what was going on, but Tom told her to wait. He'd assured her that his people and the FBI were almost ready to draw the noose on her predators. She hadn't asked for any details. She knew Tom would tell her what she needed to know, and right now, she had her hands full trying to build a new brand around a web site. It was still a long shot, but the self-heating package might be just enough to draw all of the other innovations together in one integrated leap forward. She was counting on it. She only hoped the trunk of her innovation tree was strong enough to carry the breakthroughs all the way to fruition.

In a private conversation with Goodrich before he left Dameco, Taylor asked him to keep everything he'd seen and heard under wraps until they were ready to go to market. He agreed. Then he said something she knew she wouldn't soon forget.

"I'm proud of you, Taylor. You allowed your people to discover their own greatness, then you drew them together in a common cause. That's the mark of a true leader. Brad told me why you decided to reintegrate the three innovation groups. Both moves were brilliant—the decision to separate the groups and the decision to reintegrate them. For what it's worth, I think we'll be talking about your innovation tree for many years to come. And, don't worry about the resources, we'll find the money for your advertising campaign, even if I have to fund it myself. Just keep me posted."

She said good-bye to her boss and walked to the pier to meet her children and Tom. Without fully recognizing it until now, the past several weeks had been both terrifying and transforming. In a strange sort of way, she was grateful.

As the boat came into the dock and her children waved, she wondered whether any of this would have happened if it hadn't been for the extreme circumstances. Maybe, she thought to herself, that was the real breakthrough—the greater the challenge, the greater the breakthrough, if you had the stamina to keep going.

40

CHAPTER

C asey invited Jon Chimura, whom Taylor had fired several weeks earlier, to meet him early Saturday morning at Carter-Crisp Foods. He told security that a
man by the name of Jon Chi was working on a special project
for his department. The real reason for Chimura's presence,
however, was so he could hack into the company's e-mail system without alerting Platt's people. Casey was taking a big
risk by having Chimura return, but he was the only one, because of his skill and experience, who might have a chance of
breaking into the system without being detected. With any
luck, none of the people monitoring the cameras or working in
the building on the weekend would recognize him. If anyone
did, Casey was prepared with an explanation that Chimura
was simply finishing up a special e-mail marketing project
he'd started before he was fired. It was a flimsy story, he knew,
but Chimura's new beard and glasses were enough to give
Casey hope that no one would recognize him.

By early afternoon, they'd still found no way to break into
the e-mail accounts of Taylor's people without raising red
flags. Casey, Jamison, and Chimura sat in Casey's office, with

two surveillance nullifiers in place, discussing their next moves.

"How long would it take them to discover a break-in?" Casey asked, looking at Chimura who sat across from him at the small conference table.

"They'd know immediately," he responded.

"What if they aren't monitoring?"

"Even if they're not monitoring in real time, their system would alert them. They'd know within five minutes at the outside."

"How many offices do we have left?" Casey asked, shifting his attention to Jamison.

"Taylor's and the five directors'. We've been through all the cubicles."

"Can we get in?" Casey asked.

Chimura shook his head. "Security locks. Try breaking in and they'll know it." He looked down at his Blackberry Rim 957 wireless handheld. He was receiving an emergency e-mail from the systems administrator who provided support to the consulting firm Chimura had established after leaving Carter-Crisp. He quickly tapped in his password for reading encrypted messages and waited.

"Something wrong?" Casey asked.

"I'm getting an emergency message from my systems people," Chimura said, his eyes glued to the three-inch screen. "It may mean someone's trying to enter my system."

> There have been several attempts to break into your system in the past ten minutes, two of them by the FBI. We can only keep them out for so long. Suggest we delete everything.

Chimura quickly tapped in his message and then stuffed his handheld into his jacket pocket.

> Delete and disappear.

"We've been made," Chimura said and stood up. "They picked up the diagnostics I ran. We need to get out. Now. The FBI is trying to access my files. Sooner or later, they'll make the connections." He grabbed his large equipment bag and turned for the door.

"Slow down. What are you saying?" Casey said.

"I'm telling you they know we're here and they know what we're trying to do."

"How?" Casey screamed. He went frantically to his desk and opened a large file drawer. There were so many things in his office that could incriminate him.

"You tell me. They couldn't do this unless they were already on to us."

"Hold it," Casey said in exasperation. "What exactly are you saying?"

Jamison was now standing and looking dumbfounded as he listened to the interchange between Casey and Chimura.

"The FBI is on to you and has been for who knows how long. Do what you want, but I'm disappearing. I suggest you do the same," Chimura said as he opened the door and walked out into the corridor.

Casey and Jamison looked at each other before Casey slammed the file drawer shut and grabbed his keys and wallet. "Don't go home," Casey said as he rounded the corner of his desk. "Meet me at the campus apartment in two hours, and don't bring your car. We're going underground."

The campus apartment was a love nest near UCLA that Casey rented under an assumed name. He'd shared the bachelor pad with Jamison and a few of his friends on occasion, but now it would serve as a gateway to another existence.

When he arrived at the apartment by foot, there was only one thing on his mind—revenge. No one was going to obliterate his life without paying for it.

41

CHAPTER

*E*arly Monday morning Taylor entered the offices of Zacharman Partners on Michigan Avenue in downtown Chicago, where she would be working for the next several days. Tom's people had already secured the location, making it possible for communication to flow undetected between Zacharman, Dameco, Barclays, Home-Service, and Carter-Crisp.

Taylor was ushered into Neil Zacharman's office, where he was waiting to give her a progress report on the team of eight e-business marketers, consumer advertisers, and high-tech solutions people who'd been working nonstop on the snackcity.com account ever since their first meeting Saturday afternoon. Though Zacharman had told her they'd have a timetable by this morning, she'd been more than a little anxious about his ability to deliver. Her request had been demanding: to pull off the fastest web site launch in history.

"To tell you the truth, I didn't think we could do this in anything less than two weeks, but my people, who've been in contact with Barclays, HomeService, Dameco, and Carter-Crisp all weekend, have assured me that we can begin test marketing this Friday," Zacharman said with a broad smile as he handed Taylor a one-sheet summary of the preliminary test market schedule.

"Wonderful." Taylor sat down in one of the large brown leather chairs in front of Zacharman's desk and read. It was better than she'd expected. Test marketing would begin on Friday and be finished within a week. Among the top national advertising agencies, Zacharman Partners had been hit hardest by the epidemic of dot-com deaths, but they'd also learned more than any other agency about the difficulties of marrying traditional consumer advertising with e-services marketing. And that's what she was counting on.

"Our biggest concern was fulfillment logistics—coordinating between Barclays, Dameco, HomeService, and Carter-Crisp looked like a nightmare—but your people have been fantastic. And the alliance of companies you've established seems destined for success. How did you come up with the mix of players?"

"It's a long story," Taylor sighed as she ran her fingers through her hair. "Remind me to tell you when this is over."

Zacharman looked at her curiously. "That story could have a lot of market appeal."

Taylor knew Zacharman sensed there was a lot she wasn't telling him. After all, he'd built his business and his reputation on knowing his clients well, but she was cautious. "Let's get through the test market first," she told him, and turned her attention back to the schedule.

For the next three hours, they went over the details as Zacharman called in members of the snackcity.com account team to brief Taylor and make modifications as necessary.

When they broke for lunch, Taylor met Tom and her family at Szechwan House. They had been to the Children's Museum in the morning, which Kate loved, and were going to Jeremy's favorite, the aquarium, after lunch. And clearly, Taylor thought, her mother was becoming enthralled with Tom.

Things were working out, Taylor told herself as they sat down for lunch. And the more she got to know Tom Platt, the more she liked having him around. The thought made her think of Jack, again, but she knew he would want her to be happy. She looked across the table at Tom. When their eyes met and locked, the rest of the family couldn't help but notice and smile.

After lunch Taylor went back to Zacharman Partners, and for five hours, finalized the details of the test market. That night Taylor, Tom, and her family went to a Cubs game at Wrigley Field. Sammy Sosa hit two home runs and the Cubs beat the Braves. Back in their suite at the Hyatt Regency, Kate asked if they could live in Chicago. It was a good beginning to what Taylor knew would be a long and hectic week. But her situation was anything but secure, Taylor reminded herself, the children were still under threat, and there was no guarantee the test market was going to prove successful.

The next three days were devoted primarily to creating and placing TV spots, radio bites, billboards, and newspaper and magazine ads for the six metropolitan areas that would make up the test market and, with any luck, drive thousands of people to the web site snackcity.com. Taylor's time with her family was limited, but when they got together, they played hard: dining aboard the Spirit of Chicago on Lake Michigan, Six Flags at night, the Capone's Chicago tour, Sears Tower Skydeck, Alder Planetarium, and the Bicycle Museum. Tom was working hard to make sure her children and her mother enjoyed every minute of their stay in Chicago while under his constant protection. She hoped he was enjoying some of it.

Still, Taylor worried. There had been no further information about Casey and Jamison since they disappeared, and no one could confirm who they'd been working with at Nibblers. She prayed they'd left the country. Tom continued to assure her that the FBI was doing everything it possibly could to find out, and until that time, it was best not to talk to anyone, even Goodrich.

On Friday, after beta-testing the web site in the morning, the snackcity.com web site went live with full marketing support in six major metropolitan areas—Boston, Chicago, Los Angeles, Dallas, Atlanta, and Denver. In addition to the TV commercials, radio spots, and billboards, and print ads in those markets, there were numerous other marketing support initiatives—search engine registration, topic-driven bulletin boards, e-mail, reciprocal web links—that had been put into place almost overnight (at hefty price tags). By early afternoon, the snackcity.com web site was fully functioning and already receiving almost 1,000 hits per hour.

When Taylor finally sat down to go through the web site her-self, she was delighted. It was even better than the mocked-up web pages she'd seen and approved. Barclays had designed a strikingly beautiful home page for the snackcity.com web site by artfully mixing subtle blues, greens, yellows, and reds inside a large round graphic that looked like a sliced pizza. Just above the pizza, under the Snackcity logo was the tag line: Where Snack Food Reigns. The pizza itself was divided into six pie-shaped sections, each one with its own icon and label—Create, Taste, Order, Inform, Play, and Become.

Clicking on the Create icon took you to the experimental snack center, where you could participate in developing new snack ideas; clicking on the Taste icon opened up a full range of beautifully presented and currently available snacks. You could receive samples of 10 different snacks for only $5 or five for $3; clicking on the Order icon launched you into the online snack supermarket, where you could order a wide variety of Carter-Crisp and Snackcity snacks; clicking on the Inform icon led you to a library of snack food facts relating to nutrition, ingredients, and health index ratings; clicking on the Play icon took you to Snack Heaven, where you could find contests, challenges, chat rooms, fan clubs, game rooms, and celebrity snack food secrets; clicking on the Become icon took you to City Hall on Main Street in the middle of Snackcity, where you could become an official, registered Snackcity citizen with lots of funky perks and privileges. At the center of the pizza were the words *Snackers Unite.*

Taylor was absolutely thrilled with the look, feel, and accessibility of the site. The Perspective Four group and Barclays had outdone themselves, and she quickly composed and sent an e-mail praising them for their work. Now all they needed were a few million customers who felt the same way about the web site.

For the next six days, Carter-Crisp Foods would pump $6 million in advertising into the six targeted markets. Then, on the seventh day, Zacharman would analyze the results. There had been plenty of jokes in the past few days about the six days of creation and potential curses associated with the three 6s, but everyone had been convinced that six was the right number of days, dollars, and markets. Next Friday at noon, on the seventh day, it would be time to decide whether to go forward with the full-blown, nationwide marketing campaign. Zacharman had assured Taylor that the three 6s would give them enough data to project the overall business results that could be expected from a full-blown, nationwide marketing campaign.

"There's nothing else you can do now except worry," Zacharman told her. "My people, your people, and everyone else at Barclays, Dameco, and HomeService are in the trenches. The best thing you can do is relax, get some rest, stay strategic. And, seriously, work on the alliance story. It's great PR material."

Taylor realized that her face must be showing signs of fatigue. It had been a long work-hard-play-hard week, and she was exhausted. "The only way I'm leaving is if you agree to provide me with daily updates on the test market," she said firmly.

"Agreed. Now go enjoy the rest of the day with your family," Zacharman said.

"Yes, Father," she responded playfully.

"You wait and see, you'll be grateful for my advice. Too many of my clients can't see the forest for the trees because they're afraid to leave the trees by themselves."

She liked working with Zacharman. She also trusted his judgment and promised herself she'd spend some time thinking about how to tell the story of Carter-Crisp's alliances with Dameco, Barclays, and HomeService. But it wouldn't be easy without describing all the trauma and terror she'd lived through during the past few weeks. On Michigan Avenue, Taylor hailed a cab and told the driver to take her to Wrigley Field for another Cubs game with Tom and the family.

After the game, Taylor, Tom, and her family got into a stretch limo chauffeured by two of Tom's people and drove the hundred miles to Lake Juno. A little before midnight, when everyone but the limo driver and his companion was asleep, Taylor thought about how much she was looking forward to being with her kids and her mother in the next week. She was also looking forward to spending more time with Tom.

42

CHAPTER

For six days, Casey and Jamison had been lying low in the apartment near the UCLA campus, ordering food delivered from the nearby market deli, and making preparations to leave the country with new identities and passports. Everything they needed to leave for Switzerland would be FedExed to them by Monday, but Casey had already made the decision to make one last attempt at destroying Taylor's innovation agenda. Of course, now, he wouldn't be able to assume his rightful position at the head of Carter-Crisp Foods, but he could still get several million from the sale of his stock and then Bamus would owe him. Maybe in his new life he could run one of Nibblers' operations in Europe.

On Friday afternoon, he checked the activity on four Internet sites—Barclays', HomeService's, Dameco's, and Carter-Crisp's—just as he had every few hours for the past six days. But there was something different on the Barclays site now, a banner advertising the company's new snackcity.com affiliation. He immediately clicked on the banner and went to the site. As he looked at the eye-catching graphic in the center of the home page, he was infuriated. He began touring the site and became more and more incensed with each click of the mouse. Taylor had outdone herself, he muttered, and if he didn't do something, and do it soon, she was going to propel Carter-Crisp Foods into the stratosphere, revolutionizing the entire snack food industry in the process.

Casey stood up from the computer and went into the bathroom where Jamison was dying his hair for the fourth time. "Come and take a look at the web site Taylor's been building. I'm going to the Los Angeles Athletic Club to contact Bamus. You need to track down Chimura and tell him to meet us here." He saw Jamison's skeptical expression. "Tell him to look at the web site," Casey continued. "Then tell him we'll get him out of the country and give him $200,000 in cash if he can crash it."

Wearing glasses, a straw hat, and a week-old Fu Manchu, Casey arrived by cab at the Los Angeles Athletic Club on 7th Street in downtown Los Angeles. He went immediately to the library, picked up a telephone, and punched in Bamus's number.

"We need to talk," Casey said.

"This is not a good time," Bamus returned. The last thing he wanted was to talk with Casey, especially now that the man was a fugitive. He looked down at the small red light on his telephone scrambler to make sure it was on.

"Just wanted to let you know about a new web site. Snackcity.com, Carter-Crisp's latest innovation. I'm making one last attempt to slow them down before I leave the country. If it works, you can send my proceeds to the Swiss account we've been using to fund this effort. If it doesn't work, you better make sure you've covered your tracks," Casey said.

"Either way, I'll make sure you get reimbursed," Bamus said. He didn't need Casey turning his frustration on him. "Contact me when you get settled."

"I will," Casey said. "We're in this together you know."

"Be careful," Bamus added. "Don't do anything that will jeopardize your travel plans. Where can I reach you in case—?"

Casey cut him off. "Remember my bachelor pad?"

"Yeah. I remember," Bamus said.

As soon as he hung up the phone, Casey left the Club's library, telling the host who'd been watching him from the hallway that his lunch plans had changed. He climbed into a cab and returned to his apartment.

From his office at Nibblers' headquarters in downtown Los Angeles, Bamus got on the phone to Brazil. He'd take care of Casey by funneling him enough money to keep him out of trouble, but he was through debating about Dieter. He'd already wrestled with the issue for too long. More money wasn't going to motivate Dieter, but a standing threat to Angela and her family might be enough to keep him silent. He couldn't imagine giving the order to kill someone, but if it came down to a question of self-preservation, he would do it, and make Casey the patsy.

43

CHAPTER

ieter and Angela walked along the white-sand beach just south of Recife centro, knowing they were being followed. It was late morning and they'd been discussing their situation ever since they'd watched the sun rise over the Atlantic Ocean from the balcony of their hotel room.

"We can't keep living like this," Angela said as she sunk her toes into the sand and put her arms around Dieter. For a moment, they kissed.

"The surveillance is getting worse and so is my conscience," Dieter said, as they walked again. "Taylor's plan must be working."

"They'll never leave us alone, will they?" Angela's eyes were full of fear and concern.

"I'm a threat to their secrecy, and I always will be."

"Let's get out. We could go to the Consulate this afternoon," Angela said. "No matter what happens," she whispered. "I'll always be there for you."

Dieter wiped the tears from her face. They both knew what could happen if he turned himself in for the stupid mistake he'd made several months ago of selling company secrets to Nibblers. He put his arm around her and they walked back to the hotel.

"*Nunca vai existir um outro homen na minha vida,*" Angela said, resting her head on his shoulder.

"If I offer to testify, maybe they'll be lenient," Dieter said.

Back in their room at the Hotel Atlante Plaza on Boa Viagem beach, Dieter made lunch reservations at the Churrascaria Porcão de Ipanema, located near the U.S. Consulate in downtown Recife. His plan was to make it look as if he and Angela were going out to eat. But instead, he'd appeal to the Consulate for protection as an American citizen and as an informant, whose life was in danger. He was prepared to tell them everything about the surveillance, the bribe he'd accepted, the extortion, and the physical threats on his life.

After parking in a lot near the restaurant, Dieter and Angela walked toward the U.S. Consulate located in the middle of the block. When they were 50 feet away from the entrance, three men came up behind them. They were the same three who'd interrogated Dieter on the Ihla de Comandatuba, and the same ones who'd been following them ever since.

"You're not planning to do anything stupid are you, Mr. Wilkins?" the best dressed of the three asked.

"No, are you?" Dieter turned and looked at the dark-haired man flanked by his two muscular thugs.

The Consulate's entrance was now less than 30 feet away. Angela squeezed his hand tightly. "Excuse me," he said. "But we have reservations at the Churrascaria."

"Good choice," the man said and moved closer.

It was too big a risk to run, Dieter told himself as they approached the heavy metal entrance gate and guardhouse that marked the entrance to the Consulate. He'd have to find another way. As they passed the entrance, Dieter looked at the two marines, but he knew they couldn't do anything inside the electronically controlled gate. Even if the three men dragged them away, the marines wouldn't be able to stop them. They'd been trained to be suspicious of terrorist ploys. In the best-case scenario, the marines would call the federal police, who would never arrive in time to save them.

The three men hung back as Dieter and Angela passed by the guardhouse. The distance between them was now about 8 feet. Suddenly, the exit gate, a few yards beyond the entrance, swung inward as a large group of Americans began filing out.

Dieter made his decision instantly. He locked his grip on Angela's hand and screamed, "*Vamos.*"

Angela and Dieter ran for the gate. Dieter pushed her in front of him and directly into the path of one of the exiting Americans. As they collided, Dieter pushed them both into the Consulate's inner sanctum.

Within seconds, Dieter and Angela were surrounded by marines.

"I'm an American. The three men outside are trying to kill us."

The marines immediately frisked Dieter and Angela for weapons and then restrained them until the rest of the Americans had exited through the gate and the gate was closed.

From outside the closed gate the three men began yelling that Dieter and Angela had robbed them.

One of the marines turned to Dieter. "Do you have your passport?"

Dieter immediately pulled his passport from his front pants pocket. "They're lying," he said. "I'm a U.S. citizen. This is my fiancée. Our lives have been threatened. I need to talk with the legal attaché as soon as possible."

Two marines escorted Dieter and Angela to a waiting room and stood guard while two others went to report the situation. Within 10 minutes, Dieter and Angela were ushered into the office of the legal attaché.

For the next two hours, Dieter explained how Nibblers was trying to sabotage Carter-Crisp's new product introductions so the Carter family would be forced into selling their company to Nibblers. Alexander Bamus, head of mergers and acquisitions for Nibblers, had been trying to acquire the company for several months without success, so he reverted to bribery and extortion. What Nibblers wanted, in addition to Carter-Crisp's $800 million in revenues and an innovative corporate culture, Dieter explained, were the technology patents and processes owned by one of Carter-Crisp's joint-venture partners, a German company by the name of Dameco. Dieter recounted how he'd personally developed an alliance with Dameco that gave Carter-Crisp full access to all of Dameco's patents and processes in exchange for Dameco's full access to all of Carter-Crisp's marketing and distribution relationships.

Dieter admitted to receiving $250,000 from Alexander Bamus in exchange for information on Carter-Crisp's new product plans. Nibblers had then used the information to beat Carter-Crisp to market with their own versions of the new products. The impact on Carter-Crisp's sales and profits had been devastating. When he couldn't face the reality of what he'd done any longer, he told Bamus he wanted out. He even offered to give the money back, but Bamus told him there was no way out and never would be.

Feeling trapped, he escaped to Brazil, but Nibblers found him and forced him to provide more information about what was currently happening at Carter-Crisp Foods. He explained how he'd genuinely tried to help his replacement, Taylor Zobrist, to somehow make up for what he'd done, but Bamus found a way to turn things to his own advantage. Bamus was working with someone inside Carter-Crisp Foods, probably Bob Casey, but Dieter admitted he wasn't sure. He finished by telling the legal attaché that he was willing to testify against Nibblers and Bamus, but said he wanted to get a lawyer first. He also offered to return the $250,000.

When it was over, the legal attaché communicated everything Dieter had told him to FBI headquarters in Washington, D.C. Within an hour, Alan Montgomery, FBI Chicago Bureau chief and personal friend to Tom Platt, was on the phone with the legal attaché asking questions and relaying information about the disappearance of suspects Bob Casey, Derek Jamison, and Jon Chimura. Before the FBI Chief hung up, he asked to speak to Dieter.

"This is Chicago Bureau Chief Montgomery of the FBI. Are you willing to testify?"

Dieter hesitated, not because he was unsure about testifying, but because he wasn't sure how to raise the immunity question, especially since he'd already told his story in return for government protection.

Montgomery sensed his reluctance. "We'll protect you and your fiancée, Mr. Wilkins, and your cooperation will be duly considered. I can't guarantee you immunity at the moment, but I'll work on it."

"I'm willing to testify," Dieter said.

"Get ready to give us everything you've got on Bamus."

Three hours later, Dieter and Angela were on their way to the airport, under marine protection, to catch an eight-o'clock flight to Chicago via Miami.

On the plane, seated in front of two FBI agents, Angela leaned over to Dieter and whispered, "Did we do the right thing?"

"Yes, only a lot later than we should have," Dieter said, reaching over to clasp her hand. "Just pray for immunity."

44

CHAPTER

aylor's week of vacation on Lake Juno ended when she learned that Dieter Wilkins was in Chicago being interrogated by the FBI. Tom told her that Dieter had confessed to being involved in the sabotage of Carter-Crisp's new product introductions.

"I have to talk to him," she said, her feelings of betrayal quickly turning to rage.

"He wanted out, but they threatened to hurt Angela. That's when he escaped to Brazil," Tom said.

Suddenly, she remembered the letter from David Cross and how she'd felt about the threats on her own family. She softened. "I just want to talk to him, for my own peace of mind. I need to know why he did it, and what he thinks Casey will do next." She paused. "Have they made any progress tracking down Casey or Jamison and Chimura?"

Tom shook his head. "Dieter says he didn't know who was involved from Carter-Crisp. His only dealings were with Bamus."

"Is he the one who started all of this?"

"I don't know, Taylor."

"Have they arrested Bamus?"

Tom hesitated, knowing that Taylor wouldn't like his answer. "No. But he's under heavy surveillance." He reached for her hand. "They're hoping Bamus will lead them to Casey and the others. My friend Montgomery at the FBI thinks that before Casey disappears for good, he'll make a final attempt to destroy what you're doing, out of revenge."

Taylor's body tightened with anxiety. "Is that what you think, too?"

"Yes," Tom said. "I think he'll go after the web site. We've already got a team of counterhackers looking for ways to stop someone from crashing or compromising the site."

"What about David Cross?" Taylor again looked at her kids.

"In our judgment, he's out of the picture, now that Casey has disappeared. Cross is a fee-for-service predator. I suspect Casey will be focusing his resources elsewhere, but we'll continue to take every precaution with your family. Four of my people and two FBI agents will be watching around the clock until this is over. Montgomery's serious about exposing this sort of high-level corporate extortion."

"I still want to talk to Dieter," Taylor said.

"I'll arrange it."

A few hours later, in a conference room at Zacharman Partners, Taylor met with Dieter Wilkins and two FBI agents. The FBI had agreed to the location to minimize Taylor's exposure, since she would be meeting with Neil Zacharman and his people after she finished with Dieter.

As soon as Taylor walked into the room, Dieter stood up. "Can you ever forgive me for what I've done? I never thought it would go this far. What I did was terribly wrong. I know that, and I'm truly sorry for my mistake. You're the last person I wanted to hurt."

Taylor sat down and gestured for Dieter to do the same. "You have helped us, Dieter. You sowed the seeds of our relationships with Dameco, Barclays, and HomeService. We wouldn't be where we are without you," she said.

"I also put you and your children in serious danger. I'm so sorry for that."

Taylor hesitated for a moment, then reached out and touched his forearm. "They're safe. That's all that matters," she said, as she saw the remorse in Dieter's expression. He'd been through hell and he was assuming responsibility, even if it was belated. "We've both been victimized by Bamus and Casey," she said. "All I want is to make sure they never do it again. What do you think they'll do next?"

"Leave the country," Dieter said. "But I agree with Platt and Montgomery. I think they'll try to destroy your new web site first."

"I know your only contact was with Bamus, but you worked with Casey. Tell me about them, what motivates them, how they think."

Bamus and Casey were two embittered men, he told her, resentful of authority and frustrated by their recent failures to gain the power and wealth that only CEOship could bestow. And now, in the face of exposure and new failure, their lust for power and wealth was turning into a thirst for destruction. As she listened to Dieter, she knew Casey and Bamus would go after the web site, but hacking into the snackcity.com system through some sort of Trojan horse virus, home page–defacing worm, or denial-of-service attack would never be enough for these guys. Her intuition told her they'd attempt something more destructive and permanent, and just to be sure, they'd probably wait around long enough to revel in the rubble. Taylor was absolutely confident of this. It was time to act.

As Taylor marched down the corridor toward Zacharman's office, Tom emerged from another conference room where he and Montgomery had been monitoring her meeting with Dieter.

"Better tell your FBI friends to pick up Bamus. I think they're going to strike before the end of the week," she said as she passed Tom without stopping.

"Why?"

"A woman's intuition," she said over her shoulder.

He hurried to catch up with her. "I'm sorry to be the bearer of bad news, but Bamus has disappeared."

Taylor stopped. "I thought you said he was under heavy surveillance."

"He was, until they lost him somewhere inside Nibblers' headquarters an hour ago." Tom shook his head in disgust. "The FBI's computer crime unit is all over your web site. They're already working with a team at Barclays to monitor all e-mails and e-orders for any evidence of an attached or embedded virus, or any other destructive code. They've installed Carnivore, the FBI's Internet-monitoring software, on the web site's system. Dozens of agents are in place to trace anything suspicious back to the sending computer by way of their Internet servers and administrators. We're ready for them, Taylor."

"Maybe this time they can catch them before they disappear," Taylor said. "But don't expect me to wait around holding my breath."

"What are you planning to do?"

"Tell the world a story about corporate politics, espionage, bribery, and extortion." Taylor paused and then continued. "Casey has to know that we're in the middle of a test market. He'll expect us to reach our advertising peak by the end of the week. That's when he'll strike, when he can do the most damage. I don't know what he's going to do. But I think it will involve more than hacking. He wants to destroy us, forever. I can feel it. And I intend to be ready for him."

"This is a Mozart moment, isn't it?" Tom asked. "What did you see *this* time?"

Taylor frowned. "This is hardly the time to be joking."

"I'm not joking. I'm trying to figure out what's going on inside your head. You're not making sense."

Without responding, Taylor walked into Zacharman's office. Tom followed. Zacharman was engaged at his computer and spun around in his chair when he heard them enter. "My assistant's making copies of the latest numbers," he said. "Sit down, please."

"How do they look?" Taylor asked.

"There's good news and bad news. Which do you want first?"

"The bad news," Taylor said without hesitation.

"After four days of advertising, the number of hits on the web site has only increased from one thousand to two thousand per hour. We still have two more days of advertising, but we expected the traffic to be much higher by now." Zacharman leaned across his desk. "The good news is the percentage of online purchases is substantially higher than expected— almost twenty percent." Zacharman nodded. "Unfortunately, unless the number of visitors increases dramatically, you're going to have trouble meeting your short-term sales projections."

"I'm not sure it matters anymore," Taylor said. "Your numbers only underscore the need for what I'm about to propose."

The men glanced at each other confused. Short-term financial results had been Taylor's primary business focus from the beginning. Now she was saying it didn't matter?

"Remember last week when you told me to start working on my story of how we brought Carter-Crisp, Dameco,

Barclays, and HomeService together?" Taylor asked as she looked at Zacharman. He nodded. "I've been thinking about it a lot over the past few days. Then, minutes ago, while I was meeting with Dieter, it all came together. And what you just said about the number of hits on the web site confirmed it."

"Confirmed what?" Zacharman asked, clearly impatient now.

"It's time to tell you the real reason why the FBI's here; why I'm living in a cottage on Lake Juno instead of in my condo in Marina del Rey; why my children and mother are in your screening room watching last year's best TV commercials and why I refuse to go anywhere without them; why we had no choice but to build alliances with Dameco, Barclays, and HomeService; and why there are nine, not eight, *I*'s of innovation—incremental, insightful, inventive, and ingenious are the four levels; imagine, integrate, isolate, and illuminate are the four stages; and *immerse* is the final stage and the ninth *I*. The ninth *I* is why Casey's attack on the web site could turn out to be the best thing that ever happens to us."

Suddenly, the door to Zacharman's office opened. His assistant entered carrying a stack of papers in her hands followed by Bureau Chief Montgomery. "Sorry for the intrusion," Montgomery said, "but I thought we were going to debrief in the conference room."

"We were," Tom said as he stood up.

Zacharman's assistant placed the stack of papers on her boss's desk and left.

"Sit down, Chief. I have a counterattack to propose," Taylor said as she smiled at Tom and Zacharman.

45
CHAPTER

Once Chimura and later Bamus joined Casey and Jamison in the campus apartment, they all began working around the clock on devising a destructive diversion strategy, making last-minute travel arrangements—new passports and identities for Chimura and Bamus—and finalizing their exit plan. Now, 24 hours later, they were almost ready.

Chimura sat in front of three laptop computers, typing in his code. "When snackcity.com gets linked to a network of pornography sites and we leak the story that the web site is a front for soliciting sex, the press will crucify them," he said. "By the time someone actually proves it was sabotage, the reputation of snackcity.com and the whole idea of online snacks will be irreparably damaged. This will set them back for months, maybe years. And it will certainly force the Carter family to sell early."

Casey was stone-faced. "You're sure they won't be able to trace us before we leave the apartment?"

"As soon as the links go live, we'll log off. It'll take hours for Barclays to discover what's happening, shut down the web site, and remove the links," Chimura said.

Casey shifted nervously. "What if they're monitoring us right now?"

"Impossible. Even if the FBI has already installed Carnivore on the Snackcity web site, they can only trace us after we've sent our e-mail with the pornography links attached," Chimura said irritably. "At which point, we'll be on our way to Geneva. Eventually, assuming Carnivore is as powerful as they say it is, they'll trace the e-mail to this DSL line and this apartment. That's when they'll find our computers and un-cover a hub of pornographic activity that's linked to Nathan Goodrich, Taylor Zobrist, Tom Platt, Carter-Crisp, Dameco, HomeService, Barclays, and the Los Angeles Bureau of the FBI. If David Cross can deliver the falsified victim testimonies you say he can, further implicating our friends and the FBI, the press will overdose on this story, Chimura exclaimed."

"Don't worry about Cross, he'll deliver. Just make sure we can get out of here without any surprises," Casey said.

"What exactly is Carnivore?" Bamus asked.

"We're wasting time with these questions," Chimura told him.

"All of us need to be comfortable before you send that e-mail," Bamus said, coolly. "This is not just about revenge. Its about creating a diversion big enough to get the FBI off our trail."

"Carnivore is the FBI's secret set of software programs for monitoring Internet traffic. The name was officially changed to DCS 1000. E-mails, web pages, chat room conversations, web browsing, and other signals can be monitored while going to or from a suspect under investigation. Because Carnivore's inner workings are secret, there's a lot of speculation about the actual scope of its capabilities. Some say it's much more powerful than the FBI has divulged, but regardless, if we're no longer logged on, it will take them a long time to trace us.

There's no way they could identify our location in less than 60 minutes. I guarantee it."

"How much longer do you need?" Casey asked.

"Thirty minutes of *uninterrupted* concentration and we'll be ready to hit the Send button," Chimura said.

Casey motioned to the others to follow him into the living room where four packed leather bags sat on the floor near the front door. "It's time to make our calls." He retrieved from his bag the three new cell phones he'd purchased under a false name and handed them out. "Everybody ready?"

Bamus and Jamison nodded, and took their phones into separate rooms in the apartment, leaving Casey by himself.

Casey called the Fight Against Pornography Hotline, the Cyber Tipline, and Pedo Watch. Bamus called the Coalition Against Pornography, the Abuse Prevention Network, and the Center for Children's Justice. Jamison called Children Now, Citizens Against Pornography, and Parents Against Sexual Exploitation. To each they gave the same story:

> Snackcity.com is a front for a national pornography and sexual exploitation ring. Check for yourselves in the Play and Become sections of the snack wheel on the home page at www.snackcity. com. If you don't find anything on your first try, keep trying. It's there.

Then Casey called the *New York Times* and the Los Angeles Police Department. Bamus called the *Wall Street Journal* and the U.S. Attorney General's Office. Jamison called CNN and the U.S. Marshal's Office. This time the story was slightly different.

> Taylor Zobrist, a senior executive at Carter-Crisp Foods, has orchestrated an alliance with Barclays, HomeService, and Dameco

to set up an online snack food service that serves as a front for a national pornography and sexual exploitation ring. A rebel faction inside the FBI and a private security team led by Tom Platt are providing protection. When Bob Casey and Derek Jamison from Carter-Crisp Foods, Alexander Bamus from Nibblers, and Jon Chimura from Chimura Associates uncovered the scheme, they were forced into hiding to protect themselves.

When they finished their second round of calls, Casey called David Cross and told him to go ahead with his so-called victims who'd been bribed to testify that they were solicited through the snackcity.com web site to pose for photographs and perform other sexual acts. When he ended the conversation with Cross, Casey joined his companions in the bedroom where Chimura was preparing to send his destructive e-mail.

"Have all the calls been made?" Chimura asked. The men nodded. "Okay then. Here we go."

He positioned the cursor over the Send icon and clicked on his mouse. In a few seconds, confirmation that his e-mail had been sent appeared. Then he proceeded to log off. Suddenly, Chimura began tapping violently on his mouse and then on the keyboard. "I'm frozen, it won't let me log off," he yelled.

"Cut the power," Casey ordered.

"Won't matter," Chimura whispered as he grabbed the middle computer, ripping its plug from the surge bar. "We gotta get out of here. Now!"

"What do you mean it won't matter?" Casey yelled as the four of them ran for the living room and grabbed their bags.

Chimura knelt down to stuff his laptop into the top of his bag. "They locked onto the connection. I have no idea how, but there's no other explanation. Let's go!"

When Casey, Jamison, and Bamus were in full view outside the apartment, the voice of FBI Agent Peters blared over the loudspeaker, "Drop your bags and put your hands in the air." Within seconds, more than a dozen FBI agents with weapons drawn surrounded the three men.

Casey, Bamus, and Jamison were handcuffed and escorted to an FBI van in front of the apartment complex. When the three men were inside the van, Agent Peters and two other agents entered the apartment with their firearms raised.

"You Chimura?" Agent Peters asked.

"Yeah."

"We'll need you to come with us down to the Bureau for questioning," Agent Peters said.

"I'm ready," Chimura said as he picked up his bag and followed the agents to an unmarked car in the parking garage. Chimura had sent an e-mail to the FBI 30 minutes earlier when Casey, Jamison, and Bamus began making their telephone calls, requesting immunity in exchange for full disclosure of the location and activities of the three men. He knew the FBI would eventually track him down if he didn't turn himself in, and because he wasn't one of the originators of the scheme, he knew he had a good shot at immunity. Chimura smiled as he climbed into the backseat of the car next to Agent Peters. Carnivore was good, but not as good as he was.

46

CHAPTER

"It's over," Tom said as he entered the room where Taylor, Kate, Jeremy, and Eileen were waiting. "All of them are in custody."

Taylor jumped to her feet and threw her arms around Tom. "I can't believe it."

Kate, Jeremy, and Eileen ran over to Taylor and joined in the embrace. The kids jumped up and down, chanting, "It's over, it's over, it's over."

Soon after, when the first stories linking the snackcity .com web site with pornography began hitting the streets, Taylor immediately moved into action. With the help of Zacharman Partners and the FBI, she launched the counter-attack she'd proposed in Zacharman's office. Hundreds of e-mailed and faxed press releases hit the newsrooms of every major television network, cable station, radio station, news-paper, and magazine telling the whole story, beginning with the ill-fated relationship between two snubbed, disgruntled, and, in the end, extremely vengeful corporate executives, Bob Casey and Alexander Bamus. From there, the story told of the involvement of other executives and managers— Dieter Wilkins, Derek Jamison, and Jon Chimura from

Carter-Crisp Foods and three Brazilian security professionals from Nibblers. Then it went into great detail recounting the saga of Taylor Zobrist, who had replaced Wilkins as vice president of new product development at Carter-Crisp Foods.

It was all there, documented in black and white—the sabotaged product introductions; the clandestine correspondence with Dieter Wilkins; the sagging sales and mounting pressure from the board of directors to innovate; the threats to Taylor's children that made it impossible for her to go to the authorities or leave the company; and, of course, the story of how Taylor's nine *I*'s of innovation led to the alliances with Dameco, Barclays, and HomeService and the final exposure of the conspirators.

By the time the six-o'clock evening news was airing on the East Coast, Taylor's tale of corporate corruption, mortal danger, and triumphant innovation was the lead story. Taylor sat attentively in Zacharman's private briefing room, watching the *NBC Nightly News,* along with Neil Zacharman, Chief Montgomery, Tom Platt, and her family. Turning her predators' lies against them by using the national spotlight to expose their vicious designs was the right thing to do. And it gave snackcity.com the kind of exposure she could only dream about.

When she'd proposed her plan to Chief Montgomery, Neil Zacharman, and Tom less than 24 hours earlier, she knew that some people would criticize her for using the attack on the snackcity.com web site as a means of promoting her company's new products and delivery system, but in truth, it was the only way she could see any good coming out of the bad that she, her family, and her colleagues had experienced. To use her enemies' devices to advance the very thing they were trying to destroy—growth through innovation at the Carter-Crisp Foods Company—seemed like the ultimate justice.

Her plan had almost been scrapped, however, when Chimura turned himself in over the Internet and described the disastrous effects that the e-mail would have on public opinion. The FBI had decided to intercept everything and avert the damage until Taylor convinced Montgomery that it would eventually turn out for the better for everyone if they allowed the pornography links to be established so her counterattack could be launched. Thankfully, Tom was there to lend his support.

But it was Zacharman who had first planted the seed in her mind, when he told her to work on the story of how four different companies came together to create the snackcity. com web site. Hearing Dieter Wilkins describe the natures of the men she was up against had caused the seed to germinate. Casey and Bamus had done everything to stifle, smother, and obscure any attempt by Carter-Crisp to expand and flourish. Innovation was the company's source of growth and they'd tried to stop it. Instead of allowing Casey and Bamus to shut her innovations out of the market, she'd immersed the market in everything that pertained to the breakthroughs her team had achieved, including all of the obstacles they'd overcome in the process.

The word *immerse* came back to her as it had in the conference room with Dieter. The problem facing every new product was how to position it, how to launch it, how to brand it, how to advertise it, how to build word of mouth and viral marketing, how to promote it, how to sustain it, and how to get people to try it. The secret to brand awareness and loyalty was customer immersion. Not only did customers need to be involved in every aspect of the innovation process, they needed to be immersed in the details of the story behind every breakthrough, and they needed to be given lots of opportunities to contribute themselves. Taylor knew that what she'd stumbled upon had enormous upside potential. But even she had no idea of the payoff her breakthroughs would deliver.

Within hours of the press release hitting the media, the number of hits on the snackcity.com web site had jumped past 10,000 per hour and was still climbing. Orders for snacks poured in and Zacharman Partners was besieged by press requests for interviews with Taylor Zobrist. The entire nation was being immersed in the story of her company's innovations. The terror was over, her family was safe, and Carter-Crisp Foods might now have a brilliant future.

In the days and weeks that followed, Taylor moved her family back to Marina del Rey and became consumed by the challenge of managing Carter-Crisp's meteoric growth. Dameco contracted with four outside facilities and put on two more shifts to meet demand. Barclays shifted one-third of its workforce to focus on snacks. HomeService went on a recruiting binge for more drivers. Zacharman Partners opened an office in Southern California to be closer to its number one client, snackcity.com, and Nathan Goodrich convinced the board of directors to hire Goldman Sachs to take Carter-Crisp public. The IPO, he announced, would launch a six-month transition period during which he would turn the reigns over to Carter-Crisp's next CEO, Taylor Zobrist.

Dieter Wilkins and Jon Chimura were granted immunity. Bob Casey, Derek Jamison, and Alexander Bamus were indicted on 6 counts of bribery, 11 counts of extortion, 3 counts of slander, and 2 counts of accessory assault with the intent to kill. Nibblers' three Brazilian security operatives were already serving time in a São Paulo prison. David Cross, still at large, was placed on the FBI's most-wanted list. And Tom Platt moved from his home in Chicago to an apartment in Marina del Rey so he could be closer to Taylor and her family.

47

CHAPTER

everal months later during Christmas break at the Deer Valley Ski Resort in Utah, Taylor sat at a table in the Coyote Grill across from Nan Soros, a senior editor at the *Harvard Business Review*. She looked out the window at the beauty that surrounded the crossroads of Success and Last Chance ski runs. It was about time for Tom and the kids to pass by on another downhill run, and she didn't want to miss their waves.

Because Taylor had already postponed the interview with *HBR* twice, she invited Soros to spend a couple of days with her at their Stag Lodge condominium nestled in the pines and aspens midway up Bald Eagle Mountain. They'd spent the last two mornings together, and now Soros was about to ask her final question.

A lot had happened in the months since snackcity.com became a household word. Carter-Crisp Foods had become one of the hottest Nasdaq stocks since the initial dot-com heydays, reaching $3 billion in sales and $400 million in profits by year-end through a network of alliances and acquisitions. Taylor had become one of the best-known and most respected CEOs in U.S. history, with plans to acquire and break up the beleaguered Nibblers Corporation into a network of smaller operating companies that could serve the growing demands of her company's thriving online snack food empire. Visitors to the snackcity.com web site were averaging 6 million a day (snackcity.com was the only non–search engine site on *Business 2.0*'s weekly "Internet at a Glance" top 10 rankings). More than 35 million customers had participated in snackcity.com's heralded open innovation process, helping to create a wide variety of new snacks ranging from gourmet sandwiches, pizzas, and pastries to low-calorie, low-fat nutrient bars and snacks that tasted like your favorite French, Italian, Asian, or Mexican meal. Self-heating packs of snack food had become a rapidly expanding food category with a full aisle of shelves devoted to it in most supermarkets and convenience stores.

On the personal side, Taylor and Tom were engaged to be married in May at a small chapel on Lake Juno, and the family's summer vacation had already been scheduled for the High Teton Ranch in Jackson Hole. Tom had permanently cut his consulting load by half, even though demand for his services had skyrocketed. In the fall, they planned to move into a new home in Topanga Canyon.

Taylor waved at Kate and Jeremy as they lifted their ski poles on their way to one more trip down Last Chance. Tom followed with a salute that made her laugh.

"One more question, and we'll call it quits," Soros said, and smiled at Taylor. "There have been numerous articles written about your nine *I*'s of innovation and we've discussed many of them in this interview. For executives seeking to apply the nine *I*'s in their own organizations, what is the most important piece of advice you have to share with them?"

Taylor looked out the window at the white bark of the barren aspens, the white clumps of snow on the towering pines, the white clouds in the bright blue sky, and the blanket of white on everything in between. White on white on white—

each shade contrasting with its surroundings and providing a different dimension to the spectacular beauty. "I think the most important thing to remember about the nine *I*'s is that they're nine 'eyes,' each providing different points of view, strengths, biases, and limitations. Applying the nine *I*'s is like reading nine great novels or visiting nine different countries or interviewing nine successful CEOs. Each one offers a unique view of the world and a different possibility for accelerating creative breakthroughs."

Taylor paused a moment before she continued. "Do I think we'll be using the same nine *I*'s a few years from now? I don't know. But I suspect any new *I* will result from applying the nine that we have. All I can say is they work for us right now, because they stretch the breadth and depth of our innovative imagination and, at the same time, accelerate our realization of high-quality breakthroughs. When that stops or begins to slow down, we'll be looking for new eyes."

When the interview was over and they'd said their good-byes, Taylor threw on her ski gear. There was still time before lunch, and she couldn't resist the urge to take an extra run down Last Chance.

✢ Epilogue ✢

Imagination is more important than knowledge.

Albert Einstein

To improve is to change; to be perfect is to change often.

Winston Churchill

A change in perception does not alter facts.
It changes their meaning, though—and quickly.

Peter Drucker

Change before you have to.

Jack Welch

✢ Acknowledgments ✢

I am deeply indebted to many people for their contributions to this book: to my wife Pam and our children and their spouses Jared, Aimee, Kim, Erick, and Leigh for their unusual wisdom, undying support, and constant encouragement, especially to Pam and Leigh for their tireless editing; to my mother and father for their enthusiastic reviews and enduring love; to my agent and collaborator Michael Snell for his patient mentoring and unwavering belief in my ability to become a writer; to my business partner and colleague Christopher Raia for his brilliant mind, noble character, and thorough review of the manuscript; to my fiction editor Hester Kaplan for her insight and skill in honing the manuscript; to my Wiley editor Karen Hansen for her acquisitive vision and developmental guidance; to my former HBS classmate and enduring friend Mark Hoffman for his seasoned perspective and kindly review of the manuscript for realism and value; to Larry Alexander, Airié Dekidjiev, Amy Levy, Kirsten Miller, Paula Sinnott, Tom Laughman, and others at Wiley and its subcontractors who kept the publishing wheels rolling; to Joe Cannon for his wisdom and orthodoxy; to Don Mangum for his nurturing dialogue; to Stan Varner for his view of the universe; to Michael Silva for his revolutionary mind-set; to Eric Marchant for his search to understand personality type and temperament; to Marie Rachwalski for her strong and perceptive critique; to Brent Yorgason for his indomitable spirit; to Barbara Monteiro for her vision and commitment; and to many other family members, friends, colleagues, and clients for their unconscious but invaluable input.

♣ About the Author ♣

Craig Hickman is the author or coauthor of a dozen books, among them such best-sellers as *Creating Excellence, Mind of a Manager Soul of a Leader, The Oz Principle,* and *The Strategy Game.* A partner with Provation LLC, Consultants to Senior Leadership on Organizational Innovation, he consults for major corporations around the world. He earned his B.A. in Economics from Brigham Young University and his M.B.A. from the Harvard Business School. He lives in the Mountain West.

✤ For More Information ✤

For more information and materials on *An Innovator's Tale,*
including concepts and examples, individual and organizational assessments, interactive cases and exercises, information on retreats and offsites, updates on usage and
application, and a variety of other tips and techniques for
applying the four perspectives and five stages of innovation,
go to our web site:

www.craighickman.com

Printed and bound by CPI Group (UK) Ltd, Croydon, CR0 4YY

09/06/2025

14685913-0001